TRADING POWER

TRADING POWER

The Inside Story of How the People's Mandate Was Betrayed in the 2019 Maharashtra Election

PRIYAM GANDHI-MODY

hachette
INDIA

First published in 2020 by Hachette India
(Registered name: Hachette Book Publishing India Pvt. Ltd)
An Hachette UK company
www.hachetteindia.com

SRD

ISBN 978-93-89253-75-7

Hachette Book Publishing India Pvt. Ltd
4th & 5th Floors, Corporate Centre,
Plot No. 94, Sector 44, Gurugram – 122003, India

Typeset in Sabon LT Std 10.5/15.5
by R. Ajith Kumar, New Delhi

Printed and bound in India
by Manipal Technologies Limited, Manipal

MIX
Paper from responsible sources
FSC™ C043100

For my mother, who empowers me to do things out of the ordinary, every single day. She shines light in the darkest of places, so that I can clearly see the path ahead and what I am meant to do.

For the power players in this story who agreed to divulge intricate details of the episode, regardless of how they would be perceived. They recognize that the youth of today are aware, and seek transparency and information to be able to make their own judgements.

जिकडे सत्ता तिकडे पोळी
जिकडे सत्य तिकडे गोळी;
(जिकडे टक्के तिकडे टोळी)
ज्याचा पैसा त्याची सत्ता
पुन्हापुन्हा हाच कित्ता;
पुन्हापुन्हा जुनाच स्वार
मंद घोडा जुना स्वार

Where there is power, there is gain
Where there is truth, there is a bullet
Where there are measurable profits, there is a crowd;
Power will come to those with the money
The same story will repeat again;
Once again, the old rider will ride
The horse will be slow and the rider will be blind

– Excerpted from the poem *'Sab Ghode Bara Takke'*
('Twelve Per Cent of All Horses') by Govind Vinayak 'Vinda'
Karandikar (1919–2010), Jnanpith Award-winning Marathi poet

CONTENTS

AUTHOR'S NOTE

The idea for this book did not arise from a sudden Eureka moment. As a new government, the Maha Vikas Aghadi, a tri-party alliance led by the Shiv Sena, was formed in Maharashtra in November 2019, as a dutiful voter I watched expectantly for them to bring about progress to the state. I waited for several months, attributing their inaction on various fronts to the 'settling in' period. But after several months of observing complacency, bickering and ideological confusion, I began to ask questions, like many other voters in the state – the chief among them being: Is this government competent enough to lead our state? This led me to reflect on how it was formed in the first place.

Being a political observer, I already had a bird's-eye view of the action on the ground. Although the Maharashtra assembly election of 2019 and its aftermath have received extensive national and regional media coverage, the inside story of the actual back room deals has not been revealed by any of the involved parties. Speculation was rife, especially since the involved personalities were narrating their own version of the events that played out, often peppered with heavy mud-slinging at their opposite camps, in order to please their cadre. This is when I realized that if I wanted to bring the truth to the fore, it would have to be the portions of the story that the general public, reporters, journalists, possibly even the Members of the Legislative Assembly (the MLAs) involved did not know of. It would have to be the story of the behind-the-scenes deals and secret conversations carried out through interlocutors.

Although the saga of the formation of the Maha Vikas Aghadi government features several politicians from all parties, the actual decision-making was concentrated in the hands of six powerful politicians. Thus, the information I collected by conducting several meetings with some of these protagonists forms the crux of my book. I have woven this information together with what I already knew from media stories and other sources. The events and conversations in this book have been dramatized to make the read interesting for readers. However, it is based entirely on facts. Some parts of the story might seem improbable because people are very rarely informed of the deal-making culture of politics. That doesn't make it untrue; it just means that these aspects are almost always concealed behind the garb of 'righteousness'. Optics are very important in politics, and often what is revealed to the media or happens in full view differs vastly from what goes on behind closed doors.

This account is, therefore, my attempt at narrating the untold story of what really happened in the days that followed the 2019 Maharashtra election, and, in the process, revealing how a people's mandate was blatantly betrayed by vested political interests.

PROLOGUE

ABOUT A WEEK AFTER THE MAHARASHTRA ASSEMBLY ELECTION results were announced on 24 October 2019, a letter arrived addressed to the district collector of Beed, in the central region of the state. The collector was an Indian Administrative Services (IAS) officer named Astik Kumar Pandey. The collector's personal assistant opened the letter. It was from Shrikant Vishnu Gadale, a farmer from Vadmauli village in Kej taluka, Beed. [1] A loosely translated version of the letter found its way immediately into media reports.

30 October 2019

For,

The Honourable Governor,
Maharashtra Rajya, Mumbai

To,

The District Collector,
District Collector's Office, Beed

Subject: Regarding my appointment to the chief minister's post until the Bharatiya Janata Party and Shiv Sena resolve their issues

Dear Sir,

The Shiv Sena and the Bharatiya Janata Party are yet to resolve the issue regarding the post of chief minister, which was raised after the 2019 assembly elections. Natural calamities by way of unseasonal rains have hampered ready-to-harvest crops in the state. The farmers are tense over these calamities. At a time when farmers are suffering, the Shiv Sena and the BJP are unable to resolve the issue of who will get the chief minister's post.

Hence, till the issue is resolved, the Governor should hand over the responsibility of the chief minister's post to me.

Yours truly,

Shrikant Vishnu Gadale

The last week of October 2019 had indeed seen unseasonal rains in several regions of Maharashtra, which caused widespread damage to crops like soya bean, cotton, paddy, maize, jowar, bajra, ragi and high-value horticultural varieties of plants. The regions of Konkan, Vidarbha, Marathwada and central Maharashtra suffered the most damage. This untimely calamity happened to coincide with another momentous event in the state, the Maharashtra assembly elections.[2]

While farmers across the affected regions were worrying about their very survival and toiled hard to rescue whatever they could of their produce, in Mumbai, Maharashtra's capital city and its political centre, the BJP and the Shiv Sena were struggling to come to an agreement on retaining their alliance and defining the terms of functioning as a government.

Along with the other political parties in Maharashtra, they too whipped out their top guns to have furtive discussions with each other. Leaders who had been languishing and had been away from political limelight for a long time returned from the proverbial graveyard to work out permutations and combinations that would enable them to come to power once more. As politicos walked in and out of offices and homes of leaders of opposing parties where they would otherwise not have been seen, the media, ever hungry for a scoop, kept their eyes trained on the goings-on. These engagements primarily had to do with political alignments but were often conducted under the garb of resolving 'farmers' issues' – an excuse that was propped up frequently for the benefit of the media.

The endless bickering for power annoyed the ordinary citizens of the state, but their sense of humour remained intact. Memes and jokes were exchanged on social media even as they tried to wrap their heads around the rapidly changing political equations in the state. The voters had done their democratic duty by way of diligently making their way to polling booths and casting their vote as per their choice, and in doing so had clearly communicated which leaders and parties they were choosing to be their representatives. Their votes had gone to the Mahayuti – the Shiv Sena–BJP alliance – which was formed in 1989 and first came to power in the late 1990s and then again from 2014 to 2019. Little did they know that in the days following the election their democratic opinion would stand grossly disrespected.

It was 31 October 2019, roughly a week after the assembly election results had been announced, when a newly minted MLA, the 29-year-old Aaditya Thackeray, grandson of the late Balasaheb Thackeray and son of the Shiv Sena's current chief Uddhav Thackeray, performed an act of superheroism. He led a group of the senior-most Sena leaders to the Governor of Maharashtra with a specific demand in the midst of the political upheaval in the state.

Until then, during the five years that the Mahayuti government had held office, Aaditya had played a low-key role as chief of the Yuva Sena, the youth wing of the Shiv Sena. He had never come to the forefront, talked to the media proactively or embarked on extensive *daura*s (tours) to increase party membership. Among the few issues he had aggressively taken up during the previous regime was the digitization of the Municipal Corporation of Greater Mumbai (MCGM) schools, keeping Mumbai's nightlife alive by permitting bars, restaurants and malls to stay open for 24 hours and opposing his own government's decision to construct a metro shed in the forested Aarey Colony in Mumbai on the grounds of conserving the ecology of the area. Aaditya had never, until this election, shouldered the responsibility of speaking on behalf of the Sena, especially on sensitive issues. He had always been perceived as a political heir, still very much in his father's shadow and being trained by senior Sena leaders. With his short build, rectangular spectacles and wide grin, he came across as a laid-back personality shoved prematurely to the forefront, with the big guns standing almost too close for comfort to catch him if he faltered. To close observers it would seem that the other Sena leaders were competing with him for screen space. Most of the Shiv Sena cadre, comprised of Maharashtrian men loyal to Hindutva ideologies, viewed him as a modern, left-leaning, elite prince. To a vote bank that had found resonance in the Shiv Sena's agenda of endorsing and aggressively propagating the idea of 'Marathi pride', Aaditya's millennial temperament appeared to be a complete disconnect.

Yet, on that last day of October 2019, here was Aaditya being probed by the media outside the Raj Bhavan in Mumbai about the outcome of his visit to the state's Governor. In response, the young man said, 'The meeting with the Honourable Governor was to discuss ways to provide prompt financial aid for the farmers hit by untimely rains. The current government is a caretaker government and we want to ensure that the farmers' plight is addressed.'[3]

A few days later, on 6 November 2019, with the possibility of a BJP–Sena government being formed still looking remote, Member of Parliament (MP) Ahmedbhai Mohammedbhai Patel of the Indian National Congress (INC) met with senior BJP leader Nitin Gadkari, Union Minister for Road Transport and Highways and of Micro, Small and Medium Enterprises. While Ahmed Patel is said to be the eyes and ears of INC's president, Sonia Gandhi, Gadkari, who originally hails from Nagpur and had not been particularly involved in Maharashtra's politics for the past five years, was the former national president of the BJP. Naturally, the meeting attracted media attention. On being asked, Patel was quick to clarify, 'I met Gadkariji over farmers' issues. It was not a political meeting or on Maharashtra politics.'[4] If Aaditya's meeting with the Governor was not consolation enough for the suffering farmers, the meeting between the two heavyweights should have brought them much solace and relief. Unfortunately, it was a closed-door discussion between the two and the farmers saw no immediate relief coming their way.

About 12 days after this meeting, on 20 November 2019, Sharad Pawar, veteran politician and president of the Nationalist Congress Party (NCP), had a 50-minute meeting with Prime Minister Narendra Modi. This meeting too apparently dealt with 'farmers' issues' in Maharashtra. Sharad Pawar shared with the media that he had met with the prime minister to submit a letter that contained suggestions regarding the relief efforts required for the distressed farmers. By this time, the tussle for government formation had become intense. The Shiv Sena, the NCP and the INC were carrying out lengthy rounds of discussions on multiple fronts to arrive at a Common Minimum Programme (CMP) that would be a guiding manual of sorts if the tri-party government eventually came to power.[5]

Things took a dramatic turn on 22 November 2019, the night before the BJP's Devendra Fadnavis took oath as chief minister along with Sharad Pawar's nephew Ajit Pawar, who broke away from the NCP; these two men also had a tête-à-tête supposedly on 'farmers' issues'.[6] This was the only such meeting that seemed to have an actual impact on the farmers. Within three days of the meeting, in the last week of November 2019, when the two men were at the helm of the Maharashtra government, albeit for a short time, Chief Minister Fadnavis sanctioned ₹5,380 crore as relief for the affected farmers.[7]

Much was to happen in the days that followed that would change the course of politics in the state. Yet, even as the political circus played out, the price of onions shot through the roof and the situation became grimmer as the supply of the essential commodity halved to 2.5 million quintals from the usual 5.1 million quintals in the month of November.[8] Soaring prices of onions notwithstanding, politicking for the chief minister's chair among four major parties in the state showed no sign of abatement.

1

CHANAKYA MEETS THE VIZIER

5 February 2019, 1 p.m., Matoshree, Mumbai

Uddhav and Aaditya Thackeray had been waiting eagerly for their special guest to arrive. Prashant Kishor, well known as the chief political strategist for Narendra Modi's prime ministerial campaign during the 2014 general election, was scheduled to meet them for lunch.

By 2019, Kishor had worked as a strategist for various political parties at the state and national levels. In the months preceding his meeting with Uddhav, he had been an adviser to the Janata Dal United (JDU) camp and was known to have helped Nitish Kumar, the chief minister of Bihar, form his political strategy. In the months that followed, he was credited with shaping the massive victory of then chief ministerial candidate and now chief minister of Andhra Pradesh, Y.S. Jaganmohan Reddy's YSR Congress Party in May 2019, where it won 151 out of the 175 seats in the assembly elections.

Once Kishor, dressed in his classic white kurta-pyjama, arrived at Matoshree, the residence of the Thackeray family,

Uddhav began by congratulating him on the successful work he had done for the various parties constituting the National Democratic Alliance (NDA) and also for its opponents. Before Uddhav could proceed to apprise him on his present dilemma, Kishor said, almost with prescient wisdom, 'Uddhavji, as an important NDA ally, this is the right time for you to take a stronger stand. There is a wave of displeasure among the NDA allies who feel they have been treated disrespectfully by the BJP.'

Uddhav replied, 'Prashantji, this is very true. Not only is my party unhappy with the display of such arrogance, but so also are the people of the state. It seems the BJP has forgotten that the Sena has been its older brother for all these years. We have never disregarded them or treated them as any less than us. This is causing me great discomfort. It is time to remind them of the irreplaceable role that my father, Shri Balasaheb Thackeray, played in consolidating their presence in Maharashtra.'

The BJP and the Shiv Sena had been alliance partners for about 30 years, with minor interruptions like the one in 2014, when they fought the Lok Sabha elections together but the assembly elections separately, only to reunite a few months down the line. For the most part of those 30 years, the Sena had always held the reins of power in Maharashtra. In the popular imagination, the Sena was seen as '*motha bhau*', or elder brother, and the BJP as '*lahaan bhau*', or younger brother. The year 2009 brought a twist to this relationship when, for the first time in Maharashtra's electoral history, the BJP won more seats than the Sena, albeit falling short of the numbers of the NCP–Congress combine. That was when the elder brother–younger brother equation got flipped. There were several instances before 2014 when the BJP had tried to change the status quo, but had been unsuccessful owing to Balasaheb's larger-than-life personality and, more importantly, his political guile.

Kishor fixed his black-rimmed glasses and responded, 'Maharashtra, sir, is a state which sets the trends, even in politics. Being such an important NDA ally, your actions will be looked upon as exemplary and followed by NDA allies in other states as well. You must think through every step you take. There is no doubt that the BJP and you are natural allies, tied by your loyalty to the ideology of Hindutva which the RSS [the Rashtriya Swayamsevak Sangh] has guided you in. Your friendship with Devendraji,' he continued, referring to Devendra Fadnavis, then outgoing chief minister and current leader of the Opposition (BJP) in the state, 'is also well known. However, that does not mean you let him and the BJP walk all over you. You must be more vocal about your demands and, come what may, must not bow down to pressure. There are several other options that can be considered. Have you begun a conversation with the NCP and the Congress?'

Uddhav was impressed. He looked relieved that in Kishor he had found a professional who understood his political ambitions and concerns. He immediately asked Kishor if he would provide his services to launch Aaditya in Maharashtra politics. Kishor happily agreed, saying, 'Sir, we must establish Shiv Sena as the leading NDA ally and Aaditya as Maharashtra's new hope, just as we did with Jaganmohan Reddy in Andhra Pradesh. I will try my very best to be of assistance to you in reclaiming the title of "big brother" for your party.'[1]

Mid-February 2019, 11.30 p.m., Eastern Suburbs of Mumbai

Devendra Fadnavis, Uddhav Thackeray, Aaditya Thackeray and a man who went by the initials 'GN'[2] were meeting for the third time that year to hammer out the details of the prepoll alliance between the Shiv Sena and the BJP. The BJP and the Shiv Sena had had a strained relationship over the last four years and if the alliance was to continue both sides needed clarity on various issues. At this point, it did not seem like the alliance would last, particularly because the Sena had been quite vocal in its mouthpiece, *Saamna*, as well as in several other media outlets about its intention to contest the upcoming Lok Sabha and state assembly elections alone. For the BJP, a continuing alliance with the Sena was a sure-shot formula to winning the elections. If they could hold on to it, the Opposition stood no chance. Besides, so much effort had gone into keeping the alliance intact for about 30 years. Why allow it to break now?

Twice earlier, once in February 2019 and once in January, the four men had discreetly met in different suburban hotels in Mumbai for the same purpose. In order to keep the talks fair, Fadnavis had suggested involving GN, a Mumbai-based individual known to have come to the BJP's aid in several difficult situations in the past. An engineer residing in the suburbs of Mumbai and an extremely private person, GN called himself a 'crusader against corruption'. He was known to be close to both Uddhav and Fadnavis.

During the two previous meetings, Uddhav had alluded to the issue of the chief minister's post for his party. Tonight, he raised the same demand, and this time he did not beat about the bush. 'Devendraji,' he said, 'we want rotational chief-ministership if our alliance comes to power in the assembly elections to be held later this year.'

Fadnavis remained silent, mulling over Uddhav's words. He knew it wasn't going to be possible for him to answer in the affirmative. His party would not be agreeable to this demand under any circumstance; they all knew that the Sena was not going to win as many seats as the BJP. In any case, he could not take this decision on his own. But before he consulted Amit Shah, national president of the BJP and India's Home Minister, he wanted to ensure he had a clear idea of all of Uddhav's demands. So he asked Uddhav, 'Is this your only demand?'

GN and Aaditya looked on at the two leaders engaged in this intense discussion. The tension in the room was palpable. Prior to this, when they were discussing suitable venues for the meeting, neither wanted to meet at the other's residence. They had held their ground. Sneaking around and meeting at five-star hotels was risky. The media had their eyes trained on the leaders, as did the public. The only other choice was GN's residence, tucked away in the eastern suburbs of the city, which was finally agreed upon.

Now Uddhav looked Fadnavis in the eye and said decisively, 'We also want the Palghar seat.'

The Palghar Lok Sabha constituency was formed in 2008 as a result of delimitation. It had been part of the larger area earlier called the Thane district, controlled by Sena stalwart Anand Dighe and his merry men for many years, until Dighe died in 2001. Anand Dighe was considered the Thackeray of Thane and he groomed several Sena men, including the current leader of the Sena's party legislative, Eknath Shinde. Like Balasaheb Thackeray, Dighe too never directly contested an election. His manner of exercising control over the region involved issuing threats to rival leaders and then carrying them out. Dighe still features in the majority of the Sena posters in the region, right beside the images of Balasaheb, Uddhav and Aaditya. After his death, rumours were rife that his demise was plotted by Balasaheb himself because he had grown too big for his shoes.[3]

In 2014, BJP leader Chintaman Vanga won the Palghar seat from Hitendra Thakur (chief of the Bahujan Vikas Aghadi), who had in turn won it in 2009 from Vanga by 20,000 votes.

The Shiv Sena had not contested the 2014 election since it had a prepoll alliance with the BJP and had yielded the seat to its ally. After Chintaman Vanga's death in 2018, the constituency witnessed a high-decibel by-election in May of the same year. The Shiv Sena did not wish to yield control of the region to the BJP whose popularity was slowly beginning to show in the constituency. Hence, in that by-election, the Shiv Sena and the BJP contested independently. The Shiv Sena managed to lure Vanga's son, Shrinivas Vanga, to contest on their ticket, while the BJP fielded an ex-Congressman, Rajendra Gavit, a familiar face and the state's minister for tribal development during the Congress–NCP regime from 1999 to 2014.

When the by-poll was held in 2018, the Sena was on its path to travelling solo in the upcoming elections of 2019. It had become the BJP's strongest critic in Maharashtra and virtually played the role of an opposition party while still being a part of the government. The Sena knew that if it had to fight the general elections as well as the Maharashtra elections independently, it needed to send the message to the polity that it was indeed capable of beating the grand machinery of the BJP. The BJP, on the other hand, had lost most by-elections held in Maharashtra after 2014 and by 2018 its Lok Sabha tally had also reduced to 275 from 282. It needed to boost morale within its ranks and set the tone for the general elections.

The fight between the two parties during that by-election turned into an ugly, high-stakes battle, with each desperate to win the seat that would adequately satisfy its ego. The BJP fought on the plank of 'development', reiterating how it was backstabbed by the Sena, which had stolen its candidate. The Sena contested on the emotional message of keeping Vanga's legacy alive and how it wanted to give a fitting reply to the 'the BJP's arrogance'. Eventually, it was the BJP candidate who won the by-election, by around 29,000 votes.[4]

Surprised at Uddhav's sudden and forceful demand, Fadnavis responded, 'None of these is going to be acceptable to us Uddhavji.'

Uddhav had come prepared. Adopting a passive-aggressive tone, he said, 'Devendraji, I am afraid then that this alliance cannot continue.'

This was a big declaration on the Sena's part and there was no way Fadnavis could take a decision without consulting Amit Shah, even though he knew what Shah would say. He checked his watch; it was 1.30 a.m. To the men sitting around him he said, 'Excuse me, I need to make a call to Amitbhai.' He stepped into another room to ensure privacy and rang up Shah. Shah answered the call. 'Amitbhai, Uddhav is demanding rotational chief ministership of the state and the Palghar seat. I have denied both, to which he has said that the alliance cannot continue if his demands are not met.'

At the other end of the line Shah's response came, immediate and definite. 'That is not possible. Let the alliance break.'

Fadnavis hung up the phone and went back into the room where GN, Uddhav and Aaditya were waiting. He informed them, 'Amitbhai is also of the opinion that the alliance cannot continue because we cannot concede to these demands. To be honest, we value our alliance, and any other deal except the chief ministership would have been acceptable to us.'

With that, the late-night meeting came to a close.

A few days later

A perturbed Uddhav rang up GN and informed him that he had a counter-offer for Fadnavis and Shah. 'Here are three demands from the Sena: we want the Palghar Lok Sabha seat, we want good representation in the state Cabinet and we want equal distribution of seats in the assembly elections. And, yes, one more thing, I would like Amitbhai to come to my house and make these commitments to me, after which we will immediately leave for the press-conference to announce the continuation of the alliance,' he said.

Varsha, Mumbai

GN arrived at Varsha to brief Fadnavis about Uddhav's new proposal. Having heard the terms, Fadnavis was quick to tell GN that they would be acceptable to the BJP. Good representation in the Cabinet was a demand that the party was willing to fulfil. Uddhav and his ministers had not caused any major hurdles in the functioning of the government in the previous five-year term, despite the cacophony in the media, and Fadnavis was appreciative of their cooperation. The Palghar Lok Sabha seat was not too big of a price to pay to keep the 30-year-long alliance going.

GN facilitated a conversation between Uddhav and Fadnavis immediately after, during which Fadnavis told Uddhav, 'Glad we could work out an alternative Uddhavji.'

Uddhav responded, 'Yes, it is good. I hope GN has also informed you about my invitation to Amitbhai to come by Matoshree. I believe you will also join him.'

'Yes, of course', replied Fadnavis.

'Ah good. In that case, I want to inform you beforehand that I wish to speak to Amitbhai in private for 10 to 15 minutes.'

'That should not be a problem. I will inform Amitbhai about your request,' said Fadnavis.

'Very good. We will plan to leave for the press conference together then,' said Uddhav as he hung up the phone.

18 February 2019, Matoshree, Mumbai

Amit Shah landed at Chhatrapati Shivaji International Airport in the early hours of the day. As per protocol, he was greeted by the then president of the BJP in Maharashtra, Raosaheb Danve and Chief Minister Devendra Fadnavis. The trio made their way to a five-star hotel in downtown Mumbai, accompanied by an entourage of cars filled with officers on special duty, secretaries, personal assistants and security personnel.[5]

Other members of the BJP's core team had assembled at the hotel for their scheduled meeting with Shah. They updated him on the preparations in place for the upcoming Lok Sabha elections in April 2019. Shah then had a detailed discussion with Devendra Fadnavis on what he could expect at the scheduled meeting later that evening with Uddhav Thackeray at Matoshree.

Nestled in one of the rare serene green lanes of Bandra East, Matoshree appears to be any other unassuming building in a typical Maharashtrian neighbourhood. Matoshree has been associated with *shakti*, or power, ever since Balasaheb Thackeray lived in it and formed the Sena in the 1960s. Despite being the president of the Shiv Sena, Balasaheb never contested an election and never assumed any official government position. Yet, he remained at the epicentre of Maharashtra's politics for over three decades. Since he operated only out of his home, Matoshree became an alternative power centre. In the years that the Shiv Sena and the BJP coalition was in power – some time in the late 1990s – Matoshree was the place from where Balasaheb operated his 'remote-control government'. Today, Matoshree is just one of several power centres in the state. It no longer has the grand, intimidating aura that commanded people to gather in large crowds outside the building. Its inhabitants too have been largely unsuccessful in continuing Balasaheb's unfaltering legacy to the extent that Balasaheb would have envisaged. In fact, with the new alliance that the Shiv Sena has formed since November 2019, it seems Balasaheb's biggest fear is about to come true. Balasaheb is known to have said, 'Because I am there, the party has survived... *Nahi toh sabse pehle uski bhi Congress banti* (If not for me, the party would have also become the Congress).'[6]

At his mansion, Matoshree, that evening, Balasaheb's political heir, third son and president of the Shiv Sena, Uddhav Thackeray, paced around the living room on the third floor, flanked by his wife Rashmi, his elder son Aaditya and his aide, now general secretary of the Shiv Sena, Milind Narvekar. Milind Narvekar is not a man to be trifled with in the Sena's scheme of things. Six feet tall and always attired in well-starched Western formals and classic black Oakleys, he is a towering personality. A quick learner, he is known to be a master of several skills, a significant one being his ability to make friends in high places in political parties other than his own, as well as in bureaucratic and social circles. When he decided to join the Sena in the early 1990s, his ambition was to become a *shakha pramukh*, the branch head of a party office. However, during the recruitment interview, Uddhav saw a spark in him and offered him the position of his personal assistant – a job that Milind held for over 25 years later. In 2018, he was additionally appointed as party secretary of the Shiv Sena. Apart from his networking abilities, Milind is known for his skill in crisis management. He has always been Uddhav's go-to man in difficult times, even before Uddhav assumed the post of president of his party.[7]

Narvekar enjoys a favourable relationship with Fadnavis as well. Since 2014, whenever there have been spats that the core communications teams of the two allies have failed to handle, Narvekar has been summoned to 'sort out' the problem and step in as the last resort, always at Uddhav's command. He has proven himself to be quick and effective in every instance, and is known for getting the job done. His high rate of success arises from his being politically savvy and diligent. A disciplined man, he starts his day by seven in the morning, connecting with party leaders, reading the day's newspapers and meeting a range of people, from businessmen and lobbyists to party workers and citizens who wish to connect with Uddhav. Having his ears constantly to the ground and being quick to catch any untoward rumblings has resulted in him being entrusted with the responsibility of handling Matoshree's business and financial matters, which he continues to do as efficiently as he does everything else. On that day, too, Narvekar was constantly on the phone, coordinating the arrival of Amit Shah and Fadnavis. As the time for the meeting approached, he alerted Uddhav to prepare himself.

With one son and daughter-in-law killed in a car accident, and another estranged from the family, Uddhav was Balasaheb's only offspring who could be entrusted with the job of leading the Sena after his passing. In reality, there were several other candidates close to Balasaheb who were probably more competent for the job and commanded more respect from a majority of the Sena cadre, the Sainiks. One was Balasaheb's dynamic nephew, Raj Thackeray, and the other was Balasaheb's man Friday and ex-chief minister of Maharashtra,

Narayan Rane. However, when it came to Balasaheb making a choice for his political heir, it turned out that blood was indeed thicker than water.

Uddhav, who suffers from a long-time heart ailment, had always been a quiet, soft-spoken man. He had stayed away from party affairs and seemed reluctant to occupy the throne, his serene personality totally at odds with the characteristics that gave the Shiv Sena its identity – a party known for its brash, aggressive, violent nature and history. The party's symbol, a tiger, is a brand image one would not associate with Uddhav. Rather, the understated Thackeray was known for his organizational skills and creativity (he is an ardent photographer, among other things).

After Uddhav took over the party reins in 2003, many believed that he would be unable to handle the pressure of the job and soon have to quit. Certain political pundits still believe that the Shiv Sena is in self-destruct mode as its present leaders are confused about the party's ideology and pursue short-term opportunistic goals without a long-term vision. Loyalists, on the other hand, hold on to their conviction that the party may yet be able to recapture its lost days of glory if it makes the correct political moves. However, there is certainly a consensus on the opinion that the power of the Shiv Sena has diminished considerably, as is evident from its bleak membership numbers and a significant reduction in donations to the party from the time it came under Uddhav's command.[8]

As mentioned earlier, during Balasaheb's time, Matoshree became both the Thackeray family's home and the Shiv Sena's party office. The Sena Bhavan in Dadar, which was built to be the actual party office, became a place for the rest of the Sena's working committee officials to operate from much later. At Matoshree, the ground floor thus houses several office spaces and meeting rooms of various sizes. The first floor was earlier occupied by Smita Thackeray, Balasaheb's daughter-in-law who later separated from his estranged son Jaidev. (Jaidev is now entangled in a bitter battle with his siblings over his share in the Thackeray family's wealth.[9]) With Smita having moved to her own house in Juhu, the floor remains shut on most days now. There was a time when Smita had quite a say in the affairs of the Thackeray household as well as of the Sena. Considered to be intelligent and sociable, she was close to Balasaheb. She held meetings with politicians and businessmen, and took decisions on behalf of Balasaheb – though some claimed her decisions were to the benefit of 'her own people', those in her coterie. Several Sena leaders have spoken about the role Smita played in party matters back in the day. One of them has stated, 'Smita made no bones about her political ambitions and ran a parallel government from Matoshree during the Sena–BJP regime [between 1995 and 1999]. From bureaucrats to ministers, all were at her beck and call.' However, with Uddhav and his wife Rashmi rising in prominence and Balasaheb's health deteriorating, culminating in his death, Smita was sidelined. Eventually, she was denied a Rajya Sabha ticket, and her political ambitions were cut short.[10]

About 15 minutes after Narvekar's message to Uddhav about the approaching guests, Shah's entourage arrived at the first checkpoint at Matoshree, located at the entrance of the lane in which the house stands. The security personnel on duty had been informed to let the entourage through without further stoppage at any of the remaining three checkpoints. As Amit Shah and Fadnavis disembarked from the white government-owned SUV flanked by jeeps full of officers of the Mumbai Police, Uddhav, accompanied by Aaditya and a few senior Sainiks, greeted them warmly and led them to the second floor.

Access to the second floor of Matoshree is limited to select visitors. This was the floor on which Balasaheb had resided and it remains a sacrosanct space for Sainiks. As the meeting commenced, Rashmi, Uddhav, Aaditya, Fadnavis and Shah settled on couches placed around a small coffee table. Tea and snacks were served and small talk was exchanged. Once the conversation began, Uddhav came straight to the point, 'I am glad that we were able to work out a deal. It would have been unfortunate if our alliance had broken,' he said. 'Amitbhai, allow me to lead you to my father Balasaheb's private chamber, where we can talk privately.' Fadnavis had already briefed Shah about Uddhav's intent to have a private conversation with him. Shah got up, straightened his kurta and followed Uddhav into the adjoining chamber. Balasaheb's private chamber was connected to the room they were sitting in, separated only by a wooden door. While Uddhav led Shah inside and closed the door, Fadnavis, Rashmi and Aaditya continued with small talk.

About 10 minutes later, the duo emerged and informed them that they had agreed on a fifty-fifty seat-sharing formula for the assembly elections and a good representation of the

Sena's leaders in the Cabinet. The short meeting ended there and all those present at the meeting left together for their joint press conference.

Fadnavis, Shah and Uddhav seated themselves in one car, while the others followed in separate cars.

Blue Sea Banquets, Worli

Amit Shah, Fadnavis and Uddhav jointly addressed a press conference stating that they would contest the April 2019 Lok Sabha polls together, the BJP in 25 seats and the Sena in 23. They also announced that the two parties would be in alliance while contesting for the 288 assembly seats as well. They clarified that they had decided on this stand because the people of the state wanted the ideologically similar parties to continue governing together, especially at a time when disparate parties were coming together and posing challenges.[11]

April and May 2019, Across Maharashtra

Raj Thackeray, Balasaheb's nephew, had mostly been forced to stay out of active politics for over five years. He would not have liked to, but his party, the Maharashtra Navnirman Sena (MNS) was not able to withstand the turbulent political storm that the 'Modi wave' had unleashed in 2014. The party had won just one out of the 288 seats in the 2014 Maharashtra assembly elections.[12]

Raj had built the MNS on a parochial political stand and his radical Hindutva rhetoric was clearly inherited from his uncle.

Unfortunately, it failed to compete with his cousin's Shiv Sena, which was also based on the same rhetoric. Although the party had practically become a nonentity, Raj was hardly a leader who could be ignored. His charisma, dynamism, aggression and style, mostly modelled on Balasaheb himself, continued to have a magnetic effect on the people of the state. Thus, after maintaining a low profile for one term, Raj resurfaced during the Lok Sabha campaign in Maharashtra, after a tacit understanding with Sharad Pawar that together they would break the ruling alliance's vote share.[13] The Opposition, which comprised of the NCP and the Congress, lacked a young, dynamic orator – a gap that Raj was happy to fill.

Although Raj's party did not contest any seats in the Lok Sabha elections, he campaigned like a political heavyweight. He held public rallies in crucial parts of the state, attracting large crowds, mostly made up of young voters. His rallies were different from the usual boring political gatherings. He came prepared, spoke facts and numbers, and heavily criticized Prime Minister Narendra Modi and Amit Shah. He backed his assertion that the duo and their party should not be voted in again by playing videos of Prime Minister Modi and Shah making various promises that had remained unfulfilled. His command, '*Ae laav re to video* (Hey, put on that video)…', went viral in the media.[14] Overnight, he became a star campaigner for the Opposition. His popularity ratings soared, greatly benefitting the Opposition's narrative. Many of his speeches resembled Sharad Pawar's so closely that he came to be called '*Baramaticha popat*', or the parrot of Baramati, Baramati being Pawar's seat of power.[15]

23 May 2019

The results of the Lok Sabha election were announced and the BJP–Sena combine secured 41 out of the 48 seats in Maharashtra, making it the winner by a massive margin.[16] It also became clear that Sharad Pawar's strategy to deploy Raj on the campaign trail had not yielded the expected results for the Opposition camp.

Early July 2019, 10 Janpath, New Delhi

Raj Thackeray walked into a meeting with Sonia Gandhi to discuss a possible prepoll alliance of the MNS with the NCP–Congress combine for the state assembly elections. Sharad Pawar, Raj's most recent political godfather, had given more than one hint that although he did not oppose a coalition with the MNS, the final decision would have to be the Congress's.

For the Congress, Raj's loud Hindutva rhetoric was problematic, to say the least. In addition to the ideological mismatch, Raj's party and its fortunes were standing on a thin base and the Congress simply did not have much to gain at that point from Raj and the MNS. Hence, the Congress chief opposed the alliance with the MNS, leaving Raj red-faced. [17]

Mid-August 2019, 6 Deen Dayal Upadhyay Marg, New Delhi

Devendra Fadnavis made his way hurriedly into Amit Shah's residence. The contours of Fadnavis's smiling face gave off a warm, friendly vibe. Fadnavis is a lawyer by education, and his conduct reveals him to be a sharp, witty taskmaster – characteristics that years of toiling in law school had probably instilled in him. It is exactly this polished attitude that sets him apart from most of his contemporaries. He juggles three different languages – Marathi, English and Hindi – with ease, which enables him to connect with a wide base of people. On this day, he had with him the numbers from an internal field survey conducted to assess the BJP's chances in the Maharashtra assembly elections scheduled to be held in October.

'Amitbhai, the numbers show that if we are to fight independently without our alliance partner, we may just be able to scrape past the halfway mark. The popularity of the initiatives that our party is undertaking under the leadership of Prime Minister Narendra Modi at the Centre and those at the state level is outstanding.'

Shah, dressed in his usual linen kurta and a vest, exuded power as he sat in the massive armchair at his home office. He listened carefully, characteristically looking right into the eyes of the person addressing him. He replied, 'Devendraji, we lost the opportunity to form a government in Karnataka because of only 10 seats and in Madhya Pradesh recently because of seven seats. We should not risk Maharashtra.'

'Amitbhai, as you know, they have been a difficult ally. After the Lok Sabha elections, they have stepped up the intensity of their attacks on us,' Fadnavis pointed out, referring to the Shiv Sena.

'Yes, that is true. Try to limit the number of seats they get. In your seat-sharing discussions, try not to give away over 110 seats [out of 288]. It does not bode well to let go of our ally, especially since we have contested together in the Lok Sabha elections.'

Fadnavis returned from New Delhi and briefed the core team of BJP leaders in Maharashtra about driving a hard bargain with the Sena on seat-sharing. Thereafter, several rounds of discussions took place between the BJP and the Sena leaders, but they failed to arrive at a consensus.

2

SLEEPING WITH THE ENEMY

Early September 2019, Matoshree, Mumbai

For Uddhav, the assurances given earlier of equal power-sharing had been violated when Fadnavis and his fellow BJP leaders had begun discussing the number of seats in which the Sena would be 'allowed' to field its candidates for the Maharashtra assembly elections to be held in October 2019, just six months after the Lok Sabha polls of April 2019. In the Lok Sabha elections, out of 48 seats, the BJP had fielded candidates in 25 and the Shiv Sena in 23 seats. The BJP won in 23 – registering a strike rate of 92 per cent – whereas the Sena won in 18. The Sainiks believe that it was at this time that the BJP started behaving in an arrogant and high-handed manner. And when the BJP showed no sign of honouring the equal seat-share agreement, the Sena started getting extremely uncomfortable.

The decision makers in the Sena camp knew that their strike rate of 78 per cent wasn't dismal, but they were also well aware that the success of the NDA government at the Centre was a major contributor to the Sena's win. Their political advisers had also observed that the Sena would need the BJP by their side to maintain their winning streak. At the same time, Uddhav could hardly ignore the collective deep-seated fear within his party that the BJP was eating into their vote bank, with the decline in vote share they had witnessed after 2009. After all, both parties were connected by the ideological thread of Hindutva and right-wing politics. Loyal Sainiks like Sanjay Raut had repeatedly advised Uddhav to break the alliance with the BJP and put up an independent fight in the upcoming Maharashtra assembly polls, and Uddhav knew he would have to hold his own to avoid an existential crisis within the party in the near future.

Uddhav wasn't personally inclined to keep the alliance going at this stage but, at the same time, he was reluctant to break a long-standing political relationship for the second time – especially one his father had crafted along with the BJP's suave and popular leader, the late Pramod Mahajan.

Intent on having his party fight the upcoming election on its own and taking into account the increasing disagreements between the Sena and the BJP, Uddhav had begun to give indications to the media from the beginning of 2019, most frequently through *Saamna*, that the Sena was going to fly solo.[1] In fact, to close observers, the Sena's story was becoming like that of 'the boy who cried wolf', since the same piece of news showed up in the media too regularly. This gave the impression that it had been strategically planted to extract a better deal from the BJP. In the five years that the Sena had been a part of the government alongside the BJP,

Saamna had carried more criticism of the government than information on the work it was doing for the people. One among the several issues that the Sena put the BJP government in the dock for was the matter of the Rafale aircraft deal struck by Prime Minister Narendra Modi, by supporting the Congress's accusations of corruption within the BJP.[2] The Sena was also particularly harsh while censuring the announcement of demonetization – a key action undertaken by the Modi government in 2014.[3] Moreover, it took the BJP to task for not being able to retrieve black money through whatever means necessary, as was promised during the party's election campaign in 2014.[4]

Some saw in all of this mere political posturing, while others compared the Sena to a 'nagging wife'. At one point, many were of the opinion that if the Sena had so many issues with the government and wasn't willing to take responsibility for official decisions despite its senior leaders being present in each Cabinet meeting on account of holding ministerial designations, the party would do better to simply walk out of the alliance. In 2014, Uddhav had lost face when his party, after fighting the polls independently, eventually formed an alliance with the BJP. At the time, he realized (after the NCP decided to offer outside support to the BJP) that it did indeed want to be a part of a ruling government and was not prepared to sit in the Opposition. It had thus patched up its alliance with the BJP – almost as an afterthought.

This erratic behaviour further damaged Uddhav's reputation and, as a consequence, that of the party, which had been built on one man's towering personality – his father's. He knew that while he could not lead as strongly as Balasaheb, he could also not afford to emerge from a situation like this looking like the villain of the piece. Thus, this time around, he wanted to take decisions he would stick to and not reinforce the impression that he was fickle. It was no secret that the Shiv Sena had shared a chequered past with Prime Minister Narendra Modi since his days as the chief minister of Gujarat. Uddhav had stretched the rift further by allowing his militant party to continuously criticize the prime minister's office over several policy issues. Now, if he wanted to ensure any kind of a political future for his party, he would have to walk on eggshells and make sure he made the right moves.

Amit Shah and Fadnavis knew the seriousness of Uddhav's intent to pitch the Sena independently, outside of a prepoll alliance. They knew that this was not merely a political threat. Uddhav had done it before in 2014 and had announced his intent prior to the 2019 Lok Sabha polls too. It was a well-thought-out strategy to get the BJP in a position where they would be forced to negotiate. Ahead of the Lok Sabha polls, Uddhav had begun by demanding rotational chief ministership before he had settled for the Palghar seat and equal power-sharing in the government in Maharashtra.[5]

The rumblings on the ground, too, weren't entirely promising for the BJP. Due to anti-incumbency and their handling of several crisis situations over the previous term of its government in Maharashtra, the BJP was bound to take a hit in the polls. The choice, Shah had realized, was between attack and defence, and he chose his strategy carefully as he had confidence in his party's ability to maintain its winning streak even if it meant contesting from a lesser number of seats as part of an alliance.

Meanwhile, criticism was building, especially within the BJP's allies countrywide and several sections of the media, that the party was not able to keep its allies satisfied. Such a perception, Shah knew, would have an impact on the electoral equation. He knew he would need to lose a part of this battle and appease the sulking Sena in order to project that all the NDA allies were on the best of terms.

While Fadnavis drove home a hard bargain, in the next few days, Uddhav held extensive consultations with his trusted advisers and decided that his son Aaditya would have to be fielded in this election. No one from the Thackeray family had ever contested in an election; no one had ever held any kind of government position. Uddhav himself had no direct experience heading the government or a government department. Yes, the Sena's ministers and corporators reported to him and took his input on decisions being made in matters involving the municipal corporations alongside those of the ministries they controlled. But that was no substitute for day-to-day on-the-job experience. Criticism that the Thackerays were afraid of electoral politics was mounting in the media and Aaditya needed to prove them wrong. He would have to swim with the tide.

Maharashtra chief minister's residence, Varsha

Chandrakant Patil (the BJP president of Maharashtra, inducted as such in July 2019, and then serving as revenue and public works department minister in the Fadnavis Cabinet), Sudhir Mungantiwar (then finance minister of the state of Maharashtra) and other senior state BJP leaders sat down with Fadnavis to discuss the first round of seat-sharing talks with the Shiv Sena. They seemed to be conflicted in their opinion of how hard a bargain they should drive with their friends in the Sena.

Some of those gathered did not want to hold seat-sharing talks with the Sena. Among them was Chandrakant Patil, who, on several occasions had reiterated, 'The BJP, if it fights alone, can win 200 seats.[6] However, we will fight together with the Sena. There is no question of the alliance breaking.' He and several others who were of the same opinion urged the chief minister, 'Devendraji, we already have 122 out of 288 seats. This is because we contested for all of the 288 seats in 2014. Our government has performed very well in the last five years and the public perception about us is really good. We are in any case cutting down the number of seats we're fielding candidates in. It doesn't look like we can limit the Sena to 110. We will have to give away more seats if we have to contest as an alliance. They are adamant on an equal number. Perhaps they will settle at a number between 120 and 125.'

Chandrakant Patil is an experienced politician with a strong political background that started with him being a member of the Akhil Bharatiya Vidyarthi Parishad (ABVP). He had risen in the ranks by way of nomination and had never fought electoral battles. In 2014, when he was made a member of Fadnavis's Cabinet owing to his perceived closeness to Amit Shah, he was given the public works department portfolio. As the BJP's term in office continued, he became the go-to man for all negotiations with the Shiv Sena and held all official as well as back-door talks with them, during which his diplomatic skills were on full display. Sometime mid-term, when Eknath Khadse, a potential chief ministerial candidate resigned from the Cabinet owing to charges of corruption, Chandrakant Patil was assigned a chunk of the heavy-duty departments held by Khadse, like revenue and rehabilitation.[7] A simple man, always dressed in a plain white polyester shirt, with no apparent intent to connect with the youth or the intellectual classes, 'Chandrakant Dada', as he was commonly known in political circles, made his way to commanding the kind of authority in the state that a deputy chief minister would.

However, despite the strong views of some of the top leaders regarding the alliance with the Sena, Fadnavis was not convinced about breaking the alliance. He knew Amit Shah and he were on the same page, and that he and Uddhav shared a good relationship. After all, no one other than GN, Amit Shah and himself had been party to any direct alliance discussions with Uddhav. Over the last five years, Uddhav had never tried to topple the government, regardless of how unhappy he had been. Apart from the usual bickering that was part and parcel of alliances, Fadnavis had not experienced any real issues with the Sena. The government functioned smoothly as the Sena ministers did not create a ruckus during Cabinet meetings in which important government decisions were taken. He felt that if the Sena and the BJP cobbled up a prepoll alliance, they would achieve a problem-free sweep in the elections. If left to fight alone, on the other hand, he doubted they would make the magic number of 144 seats. In the event they were not able to win the required number of seats, they would have to once again rely on Sharad Pawar's generosity for outside support, just as they had in 2014.[8] Perhaps, deep within, he also felt that the Sena could get pally with the Congress and the NCP and stitch an alliance after the polls. This was a remote possibility, but he wanted to eliminate any chance of it happening. All in all, he had made up his mind – an alliance with the Sena was easier and would bring him more peace of mind.

So, once again, he brought in his friend and expert mediator GN to lead the seat-sharing talks with the Sena. He wanted to remain in control of the situation while still dealing with the Sainiks with as much fairness as was politically possible. Apart from extracting the best bargain, another important reason to limit the number of seats given to the Sena was that Uddhav's party had not achieved the kind of electoral success the BJP had.

Navi Mumbai

The year 2019, featuring two major elections in Maharashtra, saw innumerable instances of defections among political parties that weakened the Congress–NCP combine considerably and, in turn, strengthened the Sena and especially the BJP. The BJP realized that in this atmosphere, in the run-up to the election, it would have to hold its cards close to its chest. In order to not destabilize its weak alliance with the Sena and keep the morale of its party workers high across the state, it kept its candidates list under wraps until the very last moment. The list was released just before the deadline of filing nominations on 5 October 2019.

The Shiv Sena was not so discreet in its strategy, which in retrospect could be considered to be a political mistake. Uddhav Thackeray took his party leaders into confidence by handing out AB forms to them. AB forms are documents that disclose the names of the official candidates to be fielded from each seat. Given the uncertainties and ideas of dissent that were playing on the minds of the Sena cadre, largely because of the trend of defections already underway, it perhaps would have served Uddhav better to keep the forms under wraps.[9]

In mid-September 2019, Ganesh Naik, a senior and influential NCP leader, joined the BJP. His son, Sandeep Naik, the NCP's sitting MLA from Airoli, had joined the party in August. Ganesh Naik had held sway over Navi Mumbai and Thane for over 15 years, having made use of the natural resources of the area to strengthen his political position.[10] It was a coup for the BJP and a blow to the NCP. When Uddhav circulated the AB forms within his party and the Sena workers saw that the candidates of their alliance partner, the BJP, had been given the Airoli and Belapur seats in Navi Mumbai – and, more specifically, that the Airoli seat had gone to Ganesh Naik – all hell broke loose.[11] Since the BJP could only spare one nomination for the Naik family, Sandeep immediately stepped aside, giving away his ticket to his father, who would contest from Airoli. When the Sainiks learned that Ganesh Naik would be contesting from Airoli they began to protest against the decision. The Sainiks' rage stemmed from the fact that Navi Mumbai had been where they had fought against

Ganesh Naik for years together. Now, they could not tolerate that not only had their hated rival joined their coalition partner but he had also been nominated by the BJP to a seat that the Sainiks claimed was rightfully theirs. Vijay Mane, the Sena's Navi Mumbai chief, who, in this scenario, would be forced to campaign for Naik due to the prepoll alliance with the BJP, echoed his party cadres' sentiments when he said, 'To [have to] campaign for someone like Naik, who has been hell-bent on destroying the Sena in Navi Mumbai for the past 20 years, is unacceptable. The workers do not want to do that. Around 20 years ago, Naik had forcibly removed the photo of our chief, Balasaheb Thackeray, from the building of the city's civic body. We have been in the Sena for the past two decades and our party has a firm base in this region. We would rather sit at home than campaign for Naik.'

Protesting against the move, the Sena's vice president in Thane district, the party's Navi Mumbai chief and over 200 Sainiks handed in their resignations.[12] This was the first time that the Shiv Sena was witnessing such a rebellion. Such large-scale resignations would not have been tolerated during Balasaheb's dictatorial regime; however, under Uddhav's leadership, it was clear that the party workers felt they could take more liberties.

3

RAMPING UP FOR BATTLE

24 September 2019, Mumbai

On this day, the Enforcement Directorate (ED) booked NCP chief Sharad Pawar, his nephew and former deputy chief minister, Ajit Pawar, and several other party members, bank officers and bureaucrats in a criminal case of money laundering linked to an alleged ₹25,000-crore scam in the Maharashtra State Cooperative Bank (MSCB). The ED filed an enforcement case information report (ECIR), which is the equivalent of a first information report (FIR), against Sharad Pawar, Ajit Pawar and about 80 others who were connected to the bank. The inquiry was reportedly started based on an FIR filed by the Mumbai Police's Economic Offences Wing following an order passed by the Bombay High Court in a public interest litigation. The FIR claimed that the MSCB had suffered losses due to loans given in a fraudulent manner to cooperative sugar factories.[1]

25 September 2019, Silver Oak, Mumbai

Sharad Pawar addressed a press conference at his residence, Silver Oak, stating that he would appear before the ED on Friday, 27 September, at two in the afternoon at its Ballard Estate office in Mumbai, despite receiving no summons from the ED.[2] The ED officials responded to his statement, saying that they would disallow Pawar from entering their premises to 'submit information'.[3]

In a closed-door meeting of senior NCP leaders, Pawar said, '*Mail ala ahe* (A mail has arrived). The ED is saying there is no need to come now; when we require you to come, we will let you know.'

Nawab Malik, spokesperson of the NCP, said at the meeting, 'Our strategy has worked, sir. We must push this further and reiterate that we would like to know why this inquiry has been filed in the first place.'

Pawar smiled, his eyes narrowing, accentuating the lines on his face; then he let out an impish grin as he wiped his lip with a handkerchief. He told his team, 'On what basis is the ED intervening when the court has not given any such orders?'

Malik added, 'Sir, it seems the BJP's press note accusing you in this case has been leaked to the ED, according to our sources.'

'That is unacceptable. We must take advantage of this politically. Please talk to the media and inform them that the NCP will go to the ED and demand to know on what basis this inquiry has been initiated,' said Pawar.

Later, speaking to the waiting media persons outside Silver

Oak, Nawab Malik said, 'Is the ED going to operate on the BJP's instructions? We will go to their office to ask them... Why was this case filed? We don't approve of this backhanded politicking. If we have erred, we would like the home minister of the country, Amit Shah, to tell us what we have done wrong. This is a manipulative effort to give the *rajneeti* [politics] of Maharashtra a certain direction.'[4]

In their comments to the media, ED officials said that deciding to question any person accused in a case was the prerogative of the 'investigating officer' and such a decision is taken when there are reasons to do so.[5]

Soon after disclosing the details of his visit to the ED office, Sharad Pawar urged his party workers to keep calm and not gather around the ED office, knowing full well that his workers would not stay peaceful. He also tweeted, 'I appeal to all my NCP cadre and supporters not to gather near the ED office premises. Keeping our tradition to honour the Constitution and respect our institutions, I request your cooperation with the police and other government agencies.' This came across like a well-thought-out ploy, considering that he knew that his party was planning demonstrations even as he was tweeting; his formal statement and stance were quite different from his actions on the ground.

27 September 2019

NCP workers threatened to gherao the place at the time when Pawar was to reach the ED office in Mumbai's Ballard Estate. The authorities, fearing a law and order problem, invoked the Indian Code of Criminal Procedure's Section 144, which prohibits the assembly of four or more people in a single area.

The ED officials once again urged Pawar not to come to their office and went so far as to postpone the case indefinitely. A huge public outcry arose in response to Sharad Pawar being named by the ED, with NCP supporters staging protests across the state, especially close to his home turf – Baramati. It was only after Mumbai's police commissioner, Sanjay Barve, visited Sharad Pawar at his Mumbai home and apprised him of a security problem that could arise from his impending trip to the ED office that Pawar agreed to cancel his visit.[6]

This was classic Sharad Pawar – he had once again managed to convert an adverse situation into one that was in his favour. He turned the case on its head by saying that his being named by the ED was politically motivated and that the BJP was using agencies like the ED to pressurize and weaken the Opposition. At every opportunity he got, he said it was the forthcoming assembly elections that had prompted the ED's move and that he would have been surprised if such an action had not been taken. In most of his media bytes he claimed that it was the overwhelming response that the NCP was receiving during the election campaign that was forcing the BJP to take desperate measures.

Some political analysts observed that if the strategy of the BJP–Shiv Sena partnership was to expose Sharad Pawar a few weeks ahead of the election, it had failed completely.[7] Indeed, the timing of the incident worked better for Pawar, who used the opportunity to accuse the BJP of resorting to pettiness in order to sabotage its rivals. However, according to certain investigative media reports, government officials said that if there are financial irregularities to the tune of ₹100 crore or more and an FIR is filed, the ED is compelled to act on it. The timing of the inquiry might have coincided with the announcement of the election, but the ED had acted on the orders of the court, the reports said. Several media reports from 2011 reveal that the MSCB case was a typical one of a cooperative bank going under because of mismanagement and corruption. That would mean it was not just vendetta politics, after all.[8] But Sharad Pawar used the chance to play victim and maximize the opportunity for a sympathy vote bias.

28 September 2019, Mumbai

Ajit Pawar, who was also on the board of the bank, was quick to come out in support of his party and his uncle. Minutes before addressing a press conference he made a phone call to his son, Parth.[9] Parth, 28 years of age, had fought the Lok Sabha election from Maval near Pune and lost to the Shiv Sena candidate, Shrirang Barne. On the phone call, Ajit Pawar told his son, 'Parth, I know you're working really hard to build ground in your constituency but I genuinely believe that politics is not how it used to be. It is the politics of revenge and vendetta now. We have been in politics for so many years, but have never stooped so low. What is the point of contesting elections if there is no democracy and only dictatorship? If agencies are used to harass and silence people, there is no point of being in this kind of politics. People are making allegations and filing cases. We have done so much work for the *janata*, but eventually the *janata* seems to believe these allegations. You have to make up your mind, beta, whether you are really prepared to bear all of this. If not, you should quit politics and get into business or farming. Think about it.'

Having said this, Ajit Pawar tendered his resignation from the post of a legislator and entered into a press conference where he explained his actions. He began by addressing the charges levied against Sharad Pawar. 'How can Sharad Pawar be dragged into this? Sharad Pawar has no connection with this bank. The NCP and he are being defamed because I was on the board of the bank. This is the reason I have resigned without asking him. Cooperative banks help farmers. Sometimes the help is given by going out of the way. Even the Maharashtra government gave four sugar cooperatives loans by going out of the way. How can there be a scam of ₹25,000 crore in a bank which has a deposit of ₹11,500 crore?'[10]

He added that if he had informed the party about his resignation, they would have been shocked and would have never allowed him to resign. He said that he took this step because he thought it was his right to put the interests of the party over the self, especially during a time so close to the election.

After holding the press meet, Ajit became incommunicado. Not being able to reach his nephew, Sharad Pawar, called up Ajit's son. 'Parth, have you spoken to your father? Where is he? Do you know anything about his resignation?'

Parth replied, 'Baba said your name was being dragged into the ED case for no reason. He also said that we should quit politics and take up business or farming. You were not even on the board of the bank, how can they play such vindictive politics!'[11]

Later in the day, Parth tweeted, 'It has been an emotional and difficult day for me...as a head of our family I have conveyed my father's conversation with me to @PawarSpeaks [Sharad Pawar's twitter handle].'

Sharad Pawar later assured the media, 'We Pawars have a strong bonding. I will try to understand what made him take such a decision and as the head of the Pawar family convince him [to stay in the party]. The Pawar family is known for its fighting spirit, we will fight and we will win.'[12]

The elder Pawar may have given reassurances, but reports had been doing the rounds that not everything was hunky-dory between the uncle and nephew. The question of Sharad Pawar's political heir first surfaced in 2009 when Sharad Pawar's daughter Supriya was called back to India from Singapore, where she had been living with her husband and two children. From then on, it became a thorny factor. Several NCP legislators were loyal to Ajit and in order to keep the party from splitting up after Ajit's departure Sharad Pawar knew he would have to walk on eggshells – not only did he have to build Supriya's political career but he also had to be mindful of Ajit's ambitions. However, Sharad Pawar has maintained that he is the patriarch of the family and his decisions are always considered to be the final word. Ajit follows, no questions asked. Keeping this in mind, Ajit's resignation appeared to be a calculated political move and one that had to have been blessed by Sharad Pawar in order to add more drama to the political uproar that the Pawars had orchestrated over the ED inquiry.

In other noteworthy developments that day, Sanjay Raut, the *karta-dharta* (main man) of *Saamna*, paid a courtesy visit to Sharad Pawar's Mumbai residence soon after Ajit had tendered his resignation. He stated that the reasons for his visit were 'personal', although interestingly Sharad Pawar had thanked the Sena and Sanjay Raut in his media interaction earlier in the day for their support during the recent developments.

Outside Pawar's residence, Sanjay Raut told the media, 'We have political differences with Pawar. Since Balasaheb Thackeray's time, we have been criticizing him...contesting elections against him...sometimes winning, sometimes losing. But in Maharashtra, there exists a culture whereby if anything wrong happens, we stand by each other. When Raj Thackeray was questioned by the ED [the previous month on a separate money laundering case], even Uddhav Thackeray had said positive words.'[13]

Raut's visit to Pawar raised many eyebrows in political circles. It was well known that Raut had learnt the play of politics from the best – his mentor, Balasaheb Thackeray. His actions, statements and writings made him an important and vocal pawn in Maharashtra's political game of chess, though many comments he makes pose problems for his party. For instance, after the tug of war for power ended in Maharashtra in November 2019, Sanjay Raut accused the late prime minister Indira Gandhi of having a relationship with the gangster Karim Lala.[14] This irresponsible statement did not go down well with the Congress, the Sena's new ally, and Raut had to retract his statement.[15]

India Today Conclave, Mumbai

In the run up to elections, over 35 major leaders defected from the NCP and the Congress to the BJP and the Shiv Sena. The rate of defections was so high that at the India Today Conclave held in Mumbai in September 2019, Fadnavis told journalist Rajdeep Sardesai during an interview, 'Leaders from all parties keep approaching us. They have no faith in the Opposition's existence or future any more. *Hume humaare vistaar ke bare mein sochte hue* (keeping in mind our progress), we have to evaluate whom we can take and whom we have to say "no" to.

'*Jis prakaar se Rahul Gandhiji party chalaate hain, ya Congress ki joh haalat hai, ya rashtrawadi Congress party ki joh paristhitiyaan hai, toh logon ko lagtaa hai ki in partyon ka agle bees se pachchis saal tak koi future nahi hai.* (Because of the way Rahul Gandhi runs the party, the sorry state of the Congress today, and the struggles that the NCP is going through – people feel these parties don't have a future.) They believe that if they want to continue being in politics, they must come to the BJP. The situation is so bad that if we started accepting all the leaders who came to us and kept an open-door policy, about 70 per cent of their leaders would be in the BJP today. The leadership of the opposition parties does not inspire any confidence.'[16]

4 October 2019, Mumbai

After he was convinced that the core teams of the Sena and the BJP would not be able to arrive at amicable terms for seat-sharing, Fadnavis yet again called on GN to intervene. The Sena was not willing to play second fiddle and were not ready to settle for any number less than 135 out of the 288 seats. On 22 September, Amit Shah had held a rally in Mumbai reiterating that the NDA was all set to win three-fourths of the seats in the upcoming elections. Here, he carefully avoided mentioning the Shiv Sena. He also asserted that Devendra Fadnavis was all set for a second term as chief minister.[17] With the seat-sharing talks still ongoing, Amit Shah's clear message made the Sena leaders doubly apprehensive. They wanted one of their own to become the chief minister. After all, that was the norm when Uddhav's father was alive. In order to break the stalemate, Fadnavis offered the Sena their pick from 140 seats. Out of these seats, 124 were chosen. This, he concurred, would make the Sena confident since they would be picking bases in which they were strong. His strategy worked, and after much back and forth and GN's unrelenting efforts they arrived at a deal. The Sena got 124 seats of their choice, which was more than the 110 seats that Fadnavis had originally planned to part with, as per Amit Shah's instructions. However, he felt this was the way he could save the alliance.

Once they had arrived at a consensus, Fadnavis proposed that they should jointly address the press to announce their seat-sharing arrangement. Uddhav agreed and urged Fadnavis to start with his comments, while he would, he said, join in with closing statements. To avoid any confusion, Fadnavis narrated his entire speech, word-by-word, as asserted by a source on condition of anonymity. Once Uddhav was satisfied, the two proceeded to address the press.

Fadnavis declared, 'Despite our *rajkeeya* [political] differences, it is the thread of Hindutva that binds us together. This Mahayuti brought Modiji to power in the 2019 Lok Sabha election and I am confident that we will work alongside each other to win the assembly election as well. Both of our parties have had to make compromises to ensure that the Mahayuti stays intact. We are brothers and we will share posts and responsibilities equally, like all brothers do.' Uddhav maintained a placid face while Fadnavis continued with his speech. It was only when Fadnavis welcomed Aaditya into electoral politics and announced that all the BJP candidates who were against the Sena's quota of seats would be asked to withdraw their nominations within the next two days that Uddhav nodded and smiled in agreement.

On being probed by media persons, Uddhav said, 'The seat-sharing will be 124 assembly seats (plus two council seats) for Shiv Sena, 14 for allies, and the rest for the BJP.' This was an indication that the BJP would fight from 150 seats. It also meant that the Sena would get 124 assembly seats and two Vidhan Parishad seats. Answering questions on the unequal seat distribution, Uddhav said, 'Not everything is dependent on numbers. The atmosphere in the state has changed. We have maturely taken a decision about the alliance. Instead of the elder brother–younger brother debate, the relationship of being brothers is more important. We will work together from here on.'[18]

Although Uddhav and the Sena had put up a united front at the press conference, it was clear that despite Fadnavis's assurances, talks between the two parties regarding seat-sharing and fielding candidates were still going on and were certainly not friction free. Uddhav was well aware that Fadnavis and his bosses were trying to strong-arm him. However, he too had a Plan B, for which he would have to maintain the alliance. He was okay with losing this battle in order to win the war. And, like they say, all is fair in love and war.

5 October 2019, Varsha, Mumbai

Narayan Rane, former chief minister of Maharashtra and president of the Maharashtra Swabhiman Paksha, an ally of the NDA, entered the chief minister's chamber late in the evening. Rane has an intimidating personality. For a long time, this Konkan strongman has weathered the strongest winds, first in the Sena as Balasaheb's right-hand man and then as one of the Congress's top leaders in the state. Fadnavis welcomed him warmly, although there was a battle raging in his mind. How much could he really trust Rane, he asked himself constantly.

Fadnavis had known Rane closely for over two years and had had multiple discussions with him about shifting allegiance to the BJP. Rane had been the chief minister of Maharashtra in 1999 when he was in the Shiv Sena. Six years later, in 2005, he moved to the Congress, taking several Sainiks along with him. At the time, he had openly criticized Uddhav and the new Sena leadership – thus beginning a political rivalry which would span decades.

While Fadnavis believed that Rane would be his ace draw against the Sena – because Rane knew their deepest, dirtiest secrets – he was also aware that he could not afford to enrage

Uddhav any further. Every time Fadnavis had expressed an interest in inducting Rane into the BJP, the Sena had launched vehement protests. Seeing no way around it if the Sena–BJP alliance was to hold, Fadnavis had advised that Rane resign from the Congress and form his own party, which could merge with the BJP when the time was right. He had also suggested that when such a merger happened Rane's seniority would be honoured and he would be given a plum portfolio in the state Cabinet.[19] All said and done, Rane was one of the most powerful mass leaders of the state and held considerable sway over the Konkan region. The prospect of Rane becoming powerful thus made the Sena's top brass extremely unhappy, and it also ruffled the feathers of senior BJP leaders.[20]

Owing to pressure from within his party as well as from its alliance partner, Fadnavis had so far stalled Rane's entry into the BJP. However, in March 2019, when Rane seemed to be losing his patience, Fadnavis recommended his nomination as a Rajya Sabha MP from the BJP quota. Fadnavis thought that if Rane was in New Delhi, he would perhaps be perceived as less of a threat by Uddhav and the Sena. However, the time had come to bring him back to the centre stage of state politics.

Once Rane had settled into the armchair placed opposite his, Fadnavis asked him, 'Raneji, do you think we can field your son Nitesh from the BJP in the Kankavli constituency?' Kankavli constituency was part of the BJP's share according to the prepoll seat-sharing agreement with the Sena. Nitesh Rane was Narayan Rane's younger son and the Congress MLA from the Kankavli constituency in Sindhudurg district of Maharashtra. Rane immediately agreed. 'I'll speak with him,' he said, 'but I do not think there should be any problem with that.' Then, after a pause, he continued, 'Devendraji, I have also been thinking, perhaps it is also time to merge my party with the BJP, as we had originally planned to do a couple of years ago.' Fadnavis agreed without hesitation. However, there was one problem – the Shiv Sena would have to withdraw their candidate from Kankavli. Would they adhere to that agreement?

On 3 October, Nitesh joined the BJP and on 15 October Narayan Rane merged his party with the BJP in Fadnavis's presence. When Nitesh's name was announced as a candidate for the Kankavli constituency in the second list published by the BJP it did not go down well in the Sena ranks. The Sena decided not to withdraw their candidate for the same constituency, Satish Sawant. Thus, Kankavli became the only seat for which the BJP and the Sena would take each other head-on. For both parties, winning the seat became a matter of prestige and they were hell-bent on pulling each other down. It was clear that Fadnavis had engaged Rane, a man the Sena considered their arch-enemy, and it only exacerbated the distrust the Sainiks had for the BJP. And the fact that the Sena refused to withdraw the candidature of Satish Sawant, as agreed upon during the seat-sharing discussions, aggravated the distrust for the Sena among the BJP ranks.

When the election finally took place, Nitesh Rane's massive victory with a margin of 28,166 votes in Kankavli against Satish Sawant was a hard pill for the Sena cadre to swallow. For one thing, it now became eminently clear to them that the elder brother–younger brother equation that existed between the BJP and the Sena was not about to change anytime soon, that they would not get equal status with the BJP in the state as they had desired.

October 2019, across Maharashtra

Throughout October that year, the 80-year-old Sharad Pawar traversed the entire state and spoke at over 60 rallies. He brought to the fore the problems that plagued the state, which the BJP government had failed to address. He raised the issues of agricultural distress, unemployment and the government's apathy towards the rural sector. He criticized the incumbent government's policies regarding the sugarcane industry, considered the economical backbone of western Maharashtra. He also talked about the matters affecting the larger Maratha community, rekindling the natural affection that the community had always had for him.

One of the finest politicians India will ever see, Pawar is sharp as a knife and as wily as a fox – a man who can accurately decipher which way the political current is flowing better than most other veteran politicians today. He keeps his craft of politicking separate from his personal life, an art that not many people know how to execute. This is why, regardless of associations and separations in politics, he remains socially cordial with top leaders across parties. An avid reader and deep thinker, this true-blue family man finds joy and inspiration from Indian mythology as well as history.

Circles in New Delhi as well as Maharashtra who know Pawar well say that there is no telling what Sharad Pawar thinks. Even his closest friends, family and associates possibly cannot predict his political moves. Some say that Sharad Pawar is neither anyone's permanent friend nor anyone's permanent enemy. Sharad Pawar's politics is one of adapting to change as long as it is politically convenient for him.

One instance of the Sharad Pawar brand of politics could be seen in his decision to concede the chief minister's post to the Congress thrice, in 1999, 2004 as well as in 2009, in exchange for more Cabinet berths for his party leaders. Many pundits then wondered why Pawar would lose an opportunity to occupy the chief minister's post, one which he had occupied three times in the past already. However, over the years, Pawar's intent had become clear. He wanted to expand the base of his party and having more ministers from various parts of Maharashtra would enable his party to make inroads into those constituencies.

When it comes to Pawar, it is indeed his mastery over his craft that is perhaps the most intriguing element about him. In one of the recent conversations on the alliance with the Congress, Sushil Kumar Shinde, senior Congress leader and former chief minister of Maharashtra, had told Pawar, 'We are aging and are tired. Our era of politics was different. In the current political situation, it looks difficult for our *gatbandhan* [alliance] to come back to power. Perhaps, we should merge our parties in the state.'

But Pawar did not agree. He had replied, 'I am not old and I am not tired. We shall return to power soon enough.'[21]

As things played out, Pawar single-handedly fought the poll campaign on behalf of two parties, the Congress and the

NCP – and he did it against all odds. Neither did the organized machinery of the BJP and Sena combine faze him, nor did he believe that it would be impossible to put an end to their winning streak. His alliance partner, the Congress, had given up on the state, with both Sonia Gandhi and Priyanka Gandhi skipping Maharashtra totally when it came to campaigning for the polls and Rahul Gandhi addressing only five rallies. Sharad Pawar overcame dejected leaders, numerous defections and an ED inquiry with the kind of energy that would embarrass the young guns. He stood tall through it all, proving wrong all those who were of the opinion that the era of Pawar's brand of politics was over. In doing so, he established once again that he and his party could not be written off and were still very much in the game.

October 2019, Matoshree, Mumbai

The top Sena leaders had arrived at a consensus that Aaditya Thackeray had to be fielded from the prestigious Worli constituency. They had begun preparations to field him from Worli ever since they were able to convince the NCP's Sachin Ahir to join the Sena in July 2019. Worli had been a Sena bastion since 1990, until Sachin defeated its candidate there in 2009. But the Sena got back on the Worli saddle in 2014 when Sachin was defeated by Sunil Shinde, who had done some great work on the ground for the locals and received his reward for it.

Sachin had become quite popular as an NCP leader in Worli. A young, dynamic man, Sachin hosted several social events like the Dahi Handi festival and funded extravagant Ganpati pandals in the constituency. He had built up a network of party workers and loyalists in the area. His sociable attitude and the work he did with the builder community as a minister of housing during the tenure of the previous government also made him well-regarded among the wealthy voters in the region. The Worli constituency is a contrasting mix – it has voters from across economic strata – those who reside in the massive Worli slum as well as those who inhabit the high-rise luxury towers that make up central Mumbai's skyline. Now, with Sachin in their fold and Shinde happy to make way for the newest Thackeray scion, the Sena was satisfied that they would safely retain the seat.

Back in 2006, when Sharad Pawar had fielded his daughter Supriya Sule in the Baramati Lok Sabha seat, Balasaheb had agreed not to field a candidate against her. Although they had been at opposite ends politically, Pawar and Balasaheb's personal relationship went a long way back. Uddhav expected that Pawar would return the favour now that his son, Aaditya, had entered the fray. However, Pawar's sharp sense of keeping the political advantage and his bitterness over the Sena luring away Sachin did not deter him from fielding a candidate against Aaditya – Suresh Mane, founder president of the Ambedkarite outfit, the Bahujan Republican Socialist Party (BRSP), an alliance partner of the NCP. Another possible reason may well have been his desire to conceal his real intent of eventually offering support to a Sena-led government, but that is a thought borne out only in retrospect.

Ahead of the election, the Sainiks started activating their

efficient *shakha* network, another brainchild of Balasaheb's. Balasaheb had likened the physical expansion of the Sena to a growing tree. Each polling booth was looked after by a shakha, literally a branch, and each shakha was administered by a *shakha pramukh*, or branch leader. A cluster of the *shakha*s was looked after by an *upa vibhag pramukh*, or corporator. These were then headed by *vibhag pramukh*s. The *vibhag pramukh*s, typically, were the ones directly in touch with Balasaheb or the *karya karni*s, the senior leaders. Mobilization in the Sena had followed this hierarchy for decades and was a tried and tested process of administration. Worli was a constituency of 1,23,000 voters and the Sena went ahead and gave interviews to the press declaring confidently that all candidates contesting against Aaditya would lose so badly that they would have to forfeit their deposit. They were targeting a victory by a margin of over 1,00,000 votes for Aaditya.[22]

When it came to the campaign, Aaditya performed like a seasoned politician. His style of campaigning was the kind of stuff that we see in the movies – a smartly dressed young man sporting a wide smile, waved to the crowds from an open-roof SUV, while the *karyakarta*s stood in a line to greet him with garlands. His face displayed no signs of struggle, a luxury perhaps that only privilege can provide.

18 October, Satara, Maharashtra

The NCP campaign had begun to gather momentum. At a rally in Satara, Sharad Pawar bellowed from the stage, 'People of Satara, like any other human being, I have also made mistakes.

One of those mistakes was to field the wrong candidate in the Lok Sabha polls from your constituency, who switched his loyalties.' He was talking about Udayanraje Bhonsle, who had defected to the BJP after losing in the Lok Sabha poll. Just as Pawar's speech was picking up steam, it started to rain heavily. As other leaders on the stage as well as the crowd covered their heads with umbrellas, dupattas and *kachcha*s (a piece of cloth used to wrap around the neck or head, usually when carrying a heavy object on the head), Pawar continued to roar over the microphone even as the rain drenched his clothes. The image of him dripping wet in the pouring rain went viral on social media and endeared him to estranged voters who were still on the fence, and it sealed the revival of his party in the state.

21 October 2019

On 21 October 2019, the people of Maharashtra exercised their electoral right to vote for state assembly representatives across all the constituencies in the state. Polling took place for the 288 seats of the Maharashtra assembly.

Of the 3,237 candidates who contested, 239 were women. In Maharashtra, a total of 8,98,38,267 people, including 4,28,46,822 women and 2,637 of the third gender, were eligible to vote at the 96,653 polling booths. About 61 per cent of the electorate made their way to the polling stations.[23]

Primarily in contention were two prepoll alliances – the Mahayuti, the grand alliance of the ruling BJP and the Shiv Sena, and the Maha Aghadi, the alliance of the INC and the NCP. Several small parties also fielded their candidates from different seats. Historically, the BJP and the Sena have contested together since 1989. In 1998, Sharad Pawar broke away from the INC due to differences in opinion on whether an individual of foreign origin, like Sonia Gandhi, should claim the post of prime minister in India. A year later, in 1999, he founded the NCP.

In the 1999 Maharashtra assembly elections, the NCP and the Congress contested separately, but formed a post-poll alliance when the prepoll allies, the BJP and the Shiv Sena, were not able to stake a claim to form the government. From 1999 to 2013, the NCP–Congress Maha Aghadi alliance ran the state, with the chief ministerial post always being held by a member of the Congress. However, in the 2014 elections, the NCP and the Congress fought separately.

In 2019, as per the prepoll understanding of the Mahayuti, the BJP contested in 150 seats and the Sena contested in 124. On the other hand, the Congress contested in 147 seats and the NCP contested in 121. Meanwhile, the Bahujan Samaj Party (BSP) fielded candidates in 262 constituencies, while Prakash Ambedkar's Vanchit Bahujan Aghadi contested in 235 seats. The Raj Thackeray-led MNS contested in 101 seats, the Communist Party of India (CPI) in 16, the Communist Party of India (Marxist) (CPM) in 8, the Samajwadi Party (SP) in 7 and the Socialist Workers Party (India) (SWP) in 5 seats.

The stage was now ready for the show to begin.

4

D-DAY

24 October 2019, Early Morning, Matoshree

Uddhav and Aaditya, flanked by their political advisers, party leaders and confidants, had been keeping a close watch on the numbers emerging on the television screen. The collective anticipation among those gathered was akin to that of a gambler waiting for the slot machine to arrive at the magic combination after having thrust all his money into the guzzling beast. The Sainiks had really stretched themselves in terms of financial resources for this election. As the counting advanced, it became clear to them that they had been able to maintain a number close to their 2014 count, whereas the BJP hadn't. To the Sena, this was a consolation. They kept a close watch on the NCP's and the Congress's numbers as well; permutations, combinations, additions and subtractions occupied their minds. The BJP's slipping numbers compared to 2014 was just the opportunity they had been looking for. The core committee immediately got to work and organized a press conference to be held at 4 p.m.

As for the much-awaited result from the Worli constituency, Aaditya scored a big win with 89,248 votes, while Suresh Mane finished second with 21,821 votes. All the other contestants lost their deposits. As political strategists deconstructed Aaditya's win, Mane alleged in multiple media interviews that the voters were offered ₹10,000 each for voting for the younger Thackeray and that women voters were also given saris.[1]

This seat was a make-or-break factor for the Thackeray family, one on which their political existence and power depended, and the party had left no stone unturned in ensuring Aaditya's victory here. Posters in Urdu, Hindi, Telugu and Gujarati, featuring greetings like *'Kem cho, Worli?'* (How are you, Worli?) – had been put up across the constituency, while the party elders described him as a 'visionary' and a 'game changer'.[2] Sanjay Raut had even gone so far as to say that Aaditya would be claiming the prestigious sixth floor, which houses the chief minister's office, in the ministerial headquarters, the Mantralaya.[3] Uddhav had stated in several interviews and at rallies held through September and October that it was time for him to fulfil the promise he had made his father and make a Shiv Sainik the chief minister of Maharashtra. This promise, which took centre stage in the negotiations that came about after the election results were announced, was never heard of before October 2019. Uddhav had never mentioned it while Balasaheb was alive or even after his death.

A statement of this sort reeks of dynastic politics. The chief minister's post is one accorded with a great deal of responsibility and is chosen democratically for a specific reason. The post is meant to be occupied by a highly qualified, experienced individual capable of tackling the difficult challenges that confront him or her on a daily basis. Chief ministers in India are not chosen based on promises made by sons to their fathers or vice versa. They are representatives of the people.

However, Maharashtra's voters seemed to be touched by the evocation of Balasaheb's memories and taken with the view that Uddhav was fulfilling his role as the dutiful son. Uddhav's straightforward persona and gentle mannerisms were possibly what pulled at their heartstrings. They recounted the work that the Shiv Sena had done for them over the years and stood by Uddhav, voting generously for his party to help him fulfil his father's dream. They did not give the Sena enough of a mandate to govern on its own, but they gave it enough to ensure that it was still a force to reckon with in Maharashtra's politics.

24 October 2019, across Maharashtra

While the counting was in its early stages it became clear that the Mahayuti alliance was going to hit the majority mark of 144 seats and continue to stay in power. The counting concluded with BJP's tally being 105 seats and the Sena's 56, taking the Mahayuti's total to 161. In the opposite camp, the NCP won 54 seats and the Congress 44, taking the Maha Aghadi's total to 98.

As for the small parties, the Bahujan Vikas Aghadi won three seats while the All India Majlis-E-Ittehadul Muslimeen, the Prahar Janshakti Party and the Samajwadi Party won

2 seats each. One seat each was bagged by the Shetkari Sanghatana, the Rashtriya Samaj Paksha, the Peasants and Workers Party of India, the MNS, the Krantikari Shetkari Party, the Jan Surajya Shakti and the Communist Party of India (Marxist). Independent candidates won in 13 seats.

In terms of numbers, compared to the 2014 polls, the BJP–Sena tally fell by 29 seats while the Congress–NCP alliance notched up 21 seats more, and all parties experienced a reduction in vote share. The BJP garnered about 25.6 per cent of the votes, which meant that it lost 2 per cent of vote share. The Sena saw a 3 per cent dip in its vote share, whereas the NCP and the Congress lost about 0.5 and 2 per cent respectively. The 2 per cent reduction in the BJP's vote share saw the Opposition having a field day taunting the NDA about its waning popularity.

However, the devil lay in the details when the numbers were accurately read. In 2014, the four parties had contested the election separately, fielding candidates from as many seats as they could. The increased number of candidates fattened their vote count and also contributed to a slightly better vote share. This time around, the four parties fought the election as two prepoll alliances, with each fielding their candidates from a limited number of seats. This reduced their votes as well as their vote share. Another factor that contributed to it was the percentage of the voters who made it to the poll booths – 60.46 per cent voted in the 2019 polls, 3 percentage points less than the voter turnout in 2014.

Looked at from another perspective, the BJP contested in 150 seats and won 105, which is a 70 per cent success rate.

The Sena contested in 124 seats and won 56, which amounts to a 45 per cent success rate. The NCP contested in 121 seats and won 56, achieving 44.65 per cent, and of the four parties the Congress registered the lowest strike rate, lagging behind the others at 29 per cent.

The people of Maharashtra had clearly voted for the Mahayuti to come back to power for another five years, and the next step should have been for the ruling coalition to respect the people's mandate and stake claim with the Governor of the state to form a government. However, things took an extremely dramatic turn from here on, as what initially seemed like mild bickering and politicking between all the parties involved snowballed into an intense scramble for power at the expense of the trust that people had placed in the democratic process of electing their representatives.

In retrospect it is clear that the seeds of the conflict had been sown even before the elections. On 7 October, *Saamna* had carried a story in which Uddhav was quoted as saying that if voted into power he would fulfil Balasaheb's wish and ensure that a Sainik became the chief minister.[4] Two days later, at a Dussehra rally held on 9 October in Mumbai, Sanjay Raut restated, 'There will be a Shiv Sena chief minister in the state in the times to come. Today, the Shiv Sena looks a little calm but do not go by that. Since we are in an alliance, we ought to speak carefully on some issues.'[5] These instances should have been noted as red flags for the BJP, but the party, riding high on its success – albeit less than the NDA alliance's expectation of crossing 220 seats – celebrated with much pomp all over the state. The celebrations, which would otherwise have started even as the counting of votes began, based on the expectation of a thumping victory, were slightly delayed, beginning only when the counting had almost ended. The postponement had to do with the Opposition's unexpected performance. The BJP ranks were also slightly uneasy about the lack of communication from the Sena camp.

Early Afternoon, Varsha, Mumbai

Fadnavis was glued to the television screen and, as soon as the number of seats won by the Mahayuti alliance crossed the point that indicated the Opposition had been left behind, picked up his phone and called Uddhav.

'Uddhavji,' he said, when the call connected, 'looks like we will be forming the government. *Khup, khup abhinandan*! Hearty congratulations!'

Uddhav replied, 'Yes, it does look like it, doesn't it? Thank you. Many congratulations to you too!'

'Let us meet soon. I will be travelling to Nagpur tomorrow and should be back in three to four days. We should sit together then and hammer out the details. So when do you plan to hold your press meet?' asked Fadnavis.

'I am at Matoshree right now and there is already media waiting here. We have made arrangements to hold the press meet on the ground floor. After my press meet, I will head to Aaditya's constituency,' said Uddhav.

'Ah, I see. I will be heading to the BJP headquarters now. I will hold my press meet immediately after yours,' Fadnavis informed him.

'Yes, that sounds good, Devendraji. See you soon,' said Uddhav before he hung up.

On 24 October 2019, Devendra Fadnavis made history in Maharashtra. He became only the second chief minister of the state (the first being the late Vasantrao Naik in 1972) to complete a full term and the first non-Congress chief minister to do so in Maharashtra. He also made history on another count – being the second youngest chief minister of Maharashtra at 44, second to Sharad Pawar who was 38 when he had first assumed office in 1978. In October 2014, Fadnavis had been chosen to lead the state, beating stalwarts like Nitin Gadkari and Eknath Khadse to the post. This time around, when the results were declared on 24 October 2019, a full five years later, he remained the undisputed leader. This was in spite of the fact that his party had won 17 fewer seats than it had in 2014. The Sena, on the other hand, recorded its fourth-best performance since its political existence, by winning 56 seats – 6 less than its performance in 2014, when it had contested from 282 seats.

It was said at the time that Fadnavis had systematically finished off the outliers in his party by either refusing to give them tickets or lending invisible support to the election campaigns of certain contenders who did not belong to the BJP.[6] A case in point was that of Pankaja Munde, daughter of BJP heavyweight the late Gopinath Munde, who was the woman and child welfare minister and a solid chief ministerial aspirant, yet lost to her estranged cousin, Dhananjay Munde, from the NCP. Dhananjay Munde was always believed by insiders to be close to Fadnavis and many, including Pankaja, accused Fadnavis of lending support to Dhananjay to defeat her. Very early in the term, Pankaja had been heavily embroiled in the ₹200 crore worth 'chikki scam' though she was later given a clean chit by the Anti-Corruption Bureau (ACB). Eknath Khadse, who at one point in 2014 was seen as a contender to the chief minister's post and later held over nine important portfolios, was not given a ticket to contest. A leader who was considered second-in-command to Fadnavis, Khadse had become entangled in several controversies related to the misappropriation of funds, which ultimately led him to tender his resignation from the Cabinet. An enquiry commission was set up under the ACB to investigate the alleged wrongdoings, a commonplace procedure when such incidents occur. Meanwhile the Bombay High Court, acting on a Public Interest Litigation (PIL), ordered the Mumbai Police to file an FIR against him. At this point, Khadse is said to have approached Fadnavis requesting him to direct the ACB commission to absolve him of all charges. Keeping in mind Khadse's seniority and the party's best interest, Fanavis directed the ACB commission to 'go soft' on the closure report. The ACB acted in accordance with this but the weak report was challenged by activist Anjali Damania. Eventually, it was not accepted by the high court. This was the beginning of the end of Khadse's political career with the BJP. His daughter, Rohini Khadse, was later given a ticket to contest, but lost her seat to the independent leader Chandrakant Nimba Patil, who, it is alleged, was aided with adequate resources to campaign on a large scale, leading to her defeat in the polls.[7] Since then, the BJP has won all local elections from Khadse's Muktainagar constituency in Jalgaon district.

Prakash Mehta, another BJP leader belonging to the old guard, was forced to resign as housing minister from the Fadnavis Cabinet owing to allegations of extreme irregularities indicted by the Lokayukta Commission followed by the high court.[8] He too did not get a chance to stand for election. Vinod Tawde, an aspirant for the post of chief minister, was also not given an opportunity to contest due to his alleged involvement in multiple scams.[9]

While some people openly admired Fadnavis for his prowess at dealing with the outliers, the disgruntled leaders and their supporters blamed his actions on arrogance born out of his monopoly over power. At the same time, the independence granted to Fadnavis to make decisions on ticket distribution and the fate of several leaders demonstrated how much power had been entrusted in his hands by the BJP's power centre in New Delhi. Barring only a few, Fadnavis is said to enjoy unflinching support from over half of the top-rung leaders in the party and almost all the leaders in the second rung. This is perhaps a result of his tendency to take others along and allow them to grow. Beyond the matters of the party, Fadnavis managed to expertly handle their constantly sullen ally, the Shiv Sena, over the five years he led the government. However, the way he exercised his power irked many within the BJP's inner circle since his close associates, consisting of those from outside the administration and government, were given prime posts; they made many mistakes and rubbed those they worked with the wrong way on innumerable occasions. But Fadnavis stood tall through it all. It is perhaps his ability to withstand even the harshest of storms that makes him a truly bankable leader.

However, when the results were announced on 24 October 2019, the distance that crept in between him, the Sena and his party leaders who had lost gave the impression that Fadnavis had been rendered a lonely man.

3 p.m., NCP Party Office, Mumbai

Sharad Pawar was one of the first leaders to speak to the press. When the counting had nearly ended, he told the press, 'In this assembly election, the people of Maharashtra have voted for our party in large numbers. So much so that the claim [made] by the ruling leadership (NDA) that they will win over 220 seats has absolutely failed. The people have rejected these nonsensical talks that reek of egotism. The people have given us the mandate to sit in the Opposition and we will surely live up to that mandate.' On being probed by the press about the rumours doing the rounds about the possibility of Pawar joining hands with the Shiv Sena in order to keep the BJP out of power, the NCP leader vehemently denied it. 'We have allied with the Indian National Congress and the people have asked us to be in the Opposition. We will fulfil our role as an effective opposition in Maharashtra.'

Criticizing the BJP leadership for their lack of involvement in Maharashtra before the election came along, he said sarcastically, 'The assembly elections served as an opportunity for Modiji, Shah and Fadnavis to finally get a chance to visit Maharashtra for *darshan*. I am positive that their experience as a result of this Maharashtra *darshan* will benefit the people of the state.' His attacks on the BJP did not end there, and he made sure both the prime minister and the Union home minister remained in the line of fire. 'They just sat there in their comfortable offices and homes making political predictions like astrologers who make predictions about the future,' he said. 'They don't really have much to credit themselves for in terms of their performance, which is why they constantly make personal attacks on leaders, encouraging divisive politics. People have rejected this politics of misusing central government agencies like the ED to squash opposing voices. My party did not have a problem with the scrapping of Article 370. But Modiji criticized those who opposed it, by saying, "*Jao, doob maro* (Go, drown yourselves)." This kind of language should not be used by the prime minister of our country.'[10]

Although political pundits failed to sense it then, Pawar's intention was clearly never to sit in the Opposition but play a major role in altering the political equation of the state.

In 2014, when the Sena and BJP had contested separately, Pawar's NCP had offered outside support to the BJP so that it could form the government. His offer was rejected by the BJP, and the Sena eventually came around and became a part of the government.[11] In interviews conducted later, Pawar admitted that his 2014 political move was a bid to create a further rift between the Sena and the BJP who had for the first time ended their 25-year-old alliance.[12]

4 p.m., Matoshree

Uddhav, seated next to his son, Aaditya, and flanked by senior Sena leaders like Sanjay Raut and ex-chief minister Manohar Joshi, addressed the media gathered at Matoshree. 'We thank the people of Maharashtra for trusting us and voting for us in huge numbers. The results show that the people have given us their *aashirwad* (blessings) to form the government yet again. We will continue to have the people's *aashirwad* in all our actions going forward.'

A reporter asked, 'Uddhavji, who will be the chief minister in this term?'

'Ah, a question of utmost importance,' said Uddhav. 'As you all may be aware, before the Lok Sabha elections earlier this year, in our discussions with Amit Shahji, we had decided on a fifty-fifty power-sharing formula. That formula was supposed to be applicable even for the assembly election seat-sharing, which would have meant both parties would have contested from 144 seats each. However, when certain senior leaders from the BJP came to me and said that because of some compulsions and prior commitments they would like to contest from 150 seats, I was okay with it and accepted the lower number of 124 seats.

'However, I too want to continue to expand my party and I cannot be so accommodating all the time. It is now important to remind the BJP that the time has come to implement this pre-decided power-sharing formula. The core committees of both parties will meet. If need be, Amitbhai will come down to Mumbai and decide the next steps on how that formula can be implemented. Only then will I be able to confidently say that we can stake claim to form the government. Otherwise, all roads are open for everyone.'

Another reporter asked, 'The Congress is of the opinion that if the Sena wants its own chief minister, perhaps the NCP and they can provide support. Would you be willing to consider this alliance?'

'I am sitting here peacefully. I am not power hungry. I cannot accept any such unholy, unnatural proposals. It is not in my blood,' replied Uddhav.[13]

Following the press conference, there was consensus in most circles, that Uddhav's tone had changed. It was a tone that the people of Maharashtra hadn't heard before and it was clear that it had been adopted to drive a hard bargain. Uddhav was not going to give in to pressure from the BJP easily this time. Yet, the reading was that eventually the bird would return to its flock. The Shiv Sena was, after all, bound by the same ideological parent as the – that is, the RSS. It was this ideology that motivated, held together and constantly expanded his party cadre. And, if he couldn't veer away from his party's ideology, his 56 seats didn't give him much room to play with. All he could do was to deny support to the BJP to form the government and decide to sit in the Opposition. If that happened, his cadre would be upset at losing an opportunity to be a part of the government, but they would endorse the tough stance. Balasaheb had been known to take such strong positions all the time.

Both the NCP and the Sena were vehement in their attacks on the BJP. In retrospect, this kind of attack had to be fuelled by a certain confidence that they would be able to accomplish a *satta parivartan*, a change of government. Sources later spoke of a discreet meeting between Sanjay Raut and Sharad Pawar that took place somewhere in the midst of the Mumbai–Pune expressway even as the counting was approaching its end. The duo had met just a few hours earlier in Mumbai, where Pawar had communicated to Raut that he was not able to trust the Sena's assurance that it would break away from the BJP. Raut had conveyed Pawar's mistrust of the Sena's intentions to Matoshree and the Thackerays were quick to allay his suspicions. It was imperative for Raut to inform Pawar immediately of the Thackerays' response – that after looking at the numbers, Rashmi Thackeray, better known as Vahinisaheb, had made up her mind to not support the BJP since the party had been taking advantage of 'the innocence of her husband'. Sources also confirmed that during the second meeting on the expressway, responding to Pawar's concern, Uddhav Thackeray spoke to him on Raut's phone and assured him that Raut was their official emissary and that the Sena was indeed ready to break ties with the BJP. In the new Sena leadership, it seemed like Vahinisaheb's word towered over all others. In this meeting at the expressway, it is believed that Pawar hinted to Sanjay Raut that the numbers were in favour of a *satta parivartan* and that he would actively work towards it with Uddhav.[14] This was not the first time that the Sena was playing politics being 'guided from the kitchen', as it were. Uddhav himself has pointed out that the Thackeray family is one of matriarchs.[15] Many Sena insiders have also time and again commented that Rashmi is the undeclared vice president of the party and the primary cause for the BJP–Sena break-up. A Sena leader has even gone so far as to say, 'She was clear that the Sena had to get the chief ministership and that Uddhav had to get the post. There was never any confusion, at least not in her mind, about what would happen if the deal with the NCP–Congress didn't work out.' [16]

4 p.m., BJP Headquarters, Churchgate, Mumbai

Having watched Uddhav's press interaction from the BJP headquarters at Churchgate, Fadnavis was in shock. Uddhav's 180-degree change in tone had taken him by surprise. Even as he wondered what could have prompted Uddhav's behaviour, he received a phone call from Amit Shah. 'I just watched Uddhav's press conference. I think he has something going on in his mind,' Shah told him. 'Weigh your words carefully in your media interactions and when you get a chance, please clarify that we have not made any promises of sharing the chief minister's post.'

Amidst sounds of celebrations and firecrackers outside the BJP headquarters, Chief Minister Devendra Fadnavis, looking visibly happy and exuding confidence, addressed the waiting media, flanked by the BJP state president, Chandrakant Patil, Ramdas Athawale of the Republican Party of India and a couple of senior BJP state leaders. 'I'd like to thank the people for giving our Mahayuti – the Sena–BJP alliance – an emphatic and decisive mandate,' he announced.

He added, 'If the seats contested are taken as a base, the BJP's "strike rate" this election turns out to be 70 per cent as opposed to 47 per cent in 2014. In 2014, we had won 122 seats from the contested 260. This time, we have contested 150 and won nearly 103, resulting in a better "strike rate". The vote share last time was 28 per cent on 260 seats and it is 26 per cent now on 150 seats. So, it would be wrong to say we have lost ground this time.'

At 37 minutes past 5p.m., when the press had gathered enough fodder to type up their stories, Amit Shah tweeted: 'I thank the people of Maharashtra in abundance for yet again trusting the BJP–Sena alliance. Under Modiji's leadership, our government will continue to stay committed towards the progress of the state and the service of its people.'

However, no matter how emphatic Fadnavis and Amit Shah remained in their communication that it was the Mahayuti alliance in which voters had reposed their confidence, before the counting day ended, it became clear to the people of the state that the BJP and the Shiv Sena were not on the same page or in agreement with each other.

Parties in the Opposition, such as the Congress, lost no time in commenting on this chink in the BJP's armour.

Ashok Chavan, the president of Maharashtra's Congress Party, after expressing gratitude to the people of Bhokar, the constituency he contested from, for voting in his favour yet again, remarked, 'The number of seats won by the BJP and the Shiv Sena is comparatively low compared to 2014. The BJP cannot form a government on its own. There might be new possibilities. The Congress high command should think of these options.' When asked by a journalist if by his words he meant that the Congress must offer support to the Shiv Sena, he replied, 'This is a policy decision [to be taken]. But the Congress should think of every possibility to keep the BJP away from government.'

Thus, when it became clear that the Shiv Sena was going to play it tough when it came to negotiations for government formation, the Opposition, which the voters had rejected, saw an opportunity to cast away the party that had received a clear mandate to govern.

5

PERMUTATIONS AND COMBINATIONS

25 October 2019, Mumbai

From the very next day, the Shiv Sena began to make its intent very clear. Posters depicting Aaditya Thackeray as the next chief minister surfaced in the central areas of Mumbai. These posters, put up by Sena workers, also had images of Uddhav and Balasaheb Thackeray.[1] On the following day, posters with the slogan 'Young Soch Wins' also began to crop up all over the city.[2] It was clear that Aaditya's PR team was doing its job. It was true that the Shiv Sena's 'young *soch*' (read, Aaditya Thackeray) had won – but that was only in his constituency, Worli, and in 55 other seats in the state. Political pundits wondered whether it wasn't too presumptuous for the party to stake claim for the chief ministership without having a clear majority.

26 October 2019, Matoshree

That afternoon, Uddhav held a meeting with select party leaders at his residence.

'*Saanga, kaay karaaycha?* (Tell me, what should we do)?' he asked his close team.

'Saheb, the party wants to see Aaditya as the chief minister of Maharashtra,' echoed a bunch of leaders.

'See, the path ahead is going to be hard. We are going to have to make difficult choices, at a high price even. I will assign two of you the responsibility to communicate with the BJP. Prakashji, you can speak to the media, as per our discussions,' said Uddhav.

On stepping out of the meeting, Prakash Surve, a Sena MLA, spoke to the waiting media. 'We want Aditya as our CM. This is our first and foremost demand. Before the assembly election, the BJP and our party had agreed on a fifty-fifty power-sharing formula, which we want to see implemented in letter and spirit,' he announced.[3]

27 October 2019, *Saamna* office, Mumbai

In the Sena mouthpiece, *Saamna*, Sanjay Raut runs a dedicated column called 'Rokthok'. In his column on this particular Sunday, there was a political cartoon with the Sena's symbol, the tiger, holding the BJP's lotus in its hand.[4] Raut backed up this caricature by writing in an accompanying article that the Shiv Sena should not be taken for granted, as had happened since 2014. Translated, his exact words were: 'the remote control of power in Maharashtra lies with the Shiv Sena'. His words held the open warning that this time around the Sena would not be blindly following the BJP, that it would not back down from its demands. The 'remote control' phrase had been popularly used by Balasaheb when, between 1995 and 1999, two Shiv Sena men – Manohar Joshi and Narayan Rane – had occupied the chief minister's post. It clearly implied that no matter which party representative held the title, the real power lay in his hands alone.

Raut further wrote, 'The BJP's strategy of contesting 164 seats and winning 144 of them was rejected by the voters. The election result signals the defeat of their unethical thought of increasing the tally by getting key Congress–NCP leaders to join the BJP by luring them or threatening them.'[5]

Raut seemed to have missed the fact that the Shiv Sena too had broken the Congress–NCP ranks and lured their leaders, such as Sachin Ahir, into their ranks when the need arose for them to do so. Additionally, he seemed to have overlooked the fact that winning 144 seats was not a target that the BJP had spoken about on any platform, not even at its own party meetings. The target figure that the BJP had maintained throughout the election campaign was 220-plus seats for the NDA, which would include the Sena's seats as well. Keeping these numbers in mind, the NDA performance was at about 170-plus, which was considerably less than what they had all hoped for. This meant that not only was the BJP's performance below par, but the Shiv Sena's was too.

In the days to come, more such unfounded statements were made, both in *Saamna* and to the press, that did more harm to his party than good. It appeared to observers that the Sena did not want to stop such statements from being made and some even believed that the party was encouraging them. A couple of months later, in February 2020, Rashmi Thackeray took over the role as editor-in-chief of *Saamna*. Rashmi Thackeray has been a force to reckon with following Balasaheb's death. A lady with immense political acumen, she has always been advising her husband and son behind the scenes. Under Raut's leadership *Saamna* suffered a steadily declining readership with no signs of revival. In fact, in 2019, it did not make it to the list of the top five Marathi print dailies extensively read according to the Indian Readership Survey.[6]

Late Night, a Few Days after the Results, Matoshree

Ashok Chavan and Prithviraj Chavan, both former chief ministers of Maharashtra and hardcore Congressmen, arrived at Uddhav's residence. This wasn't the first time the two men had called on Uddhav. They had frequently held closed-door meetings with him before the Assembly polls as well. However, tonight's meeting was significant. Ashok Chavan said, 'Uddhavji, the numbers aren't the best, but they look good. They show that the BJP has lost some of their popularity. It is an opportune moment for us. We believe that we can convince Soniaji to support a Sena-led government.'

'That's fantastic news. Please keep me updated. I am scheduled to hold talks with the BJP soon. So please act as fast as you can,' Uddhav requested.

Around midnight, on the same day, Uddhav held a meeting with his trusted lieutenants to inform them of the Congress's stand. For a Sena-led government to be made possible, they would have to have support from the Congress as well as the

NCP. But the crucial question was: How much trust could he place in Sharad Pawar?

Every person in the room was aware that the electoral verdict was not in the Sena's favour. Every person in the room also knew that the BJP would need support from at least one other party to get to the magic number of 144 seats to form government. The BJP already had 105 seats, and adding the independents and smaller parties, it could possibly get the number up to 120. The options for the BJP in the event that the Sena refused to support it would be to either engineer a split in one of the three parties – the Shiv Sena, the Congress or the NCP – or strike a deal for outside support where one of these three parties would walk out during the trust vote in the assembly.

The rule during a trust vote is that for a party to win, it has to enjoy the support of half the MLAs present in the assembly. If a party were to stage a walkout, the total number of MLAs would reduce, thereby spoiling the chances of getting to the halfway mark. Sharad Pawar had offered outside support of a similar nature to the BJP in 2014. There was no reason to believe he wouldn't do it again, except that he had been talking to the Sena on the side. His conversations had started long before the Lok Sabha polls in order to craft strategies to ensure that the BJP was thrown out of power.

27 October 2019, Diwali, Varsha

Fadnavis's team had organized a dinner for the media on account of the festive season. Fadnavis emerged from his bungalow to offer Diwali greetings. In an informal discussion, when asked by media persons if he believed he would remain the chief minister for the entire term, he had felt it necessary to clarify the BJP's stand, keeping in mind Amit Shah's directions. He had said, 'No rotational chief ministerial post has been promised to the Shiv Sena. There is no doubt that I will continue to hold the chief minister's position for another five years.' His statement was widely reported in the media.[7]

28 October 2019

Talks had been scheduled to take place between Uddhav and Fadnavis the day after Diwali, but Uddhav cancelled the meeting. After what he had heard reported the day before, he was in no mood to speak to Fadnavis. Besides, his meeting with Ashok Chavan and Prithviraj Chavan, during which they had informed him about their seeking Sonia Gandhi's nod to support a government led by him, encouraged him to wait until he had clearer answers from the Congress.

That night, however, he received a message from Chavan that Sonia was adamant about not supporting the Sena due to ideological differences. They were still going to try to convince her, Chavan said plainly, but her close coterie in New Delhi was not keen on supporting a Sena-led government.

29 October 2019, Sena Bhavan, Dadar

At the legislative party meet held at Sena Bhavan in Dadar the next day, Uddhav communicated to his party members his displeasure over Fadnavis's statement made on Diwali and assured his MLAs that he would not back down from his demands.

The Shiv Sena elected old-timer Eknath Shinde as its legislative party leader. Since 2014, Shinde had been in charge of the day-to-day functioning of the government and coordination with the BJP. He was the public works department (MSRDC) minister and managed the Shiv Sena's role in Cabinet meetings and interdepartmental affairs.

Later that evening, regardless of the disappointing news from the Congress leaders, Sanjay Raut visited Sharad Pawar at the latter's residence. The Sena had officially begun to explore other partnerships. Even if it could not wing it, it needed to put up a show of confidence. The party leaders probably felt that the pressure their parallel talks created would compel the BJP to succumb to their demands.

Later in the Evening, Varsha

Confused about Uddhav cancelling their scheduled appointment the day after Diwali and the strong anti-BJP statements the Sena chief had made at the party's legislative meet earlier in the day, which made its way immediately to the news channels,[8] Fadnavis called GN, the interlocutor who had facilitated their alliance talks both before the Lok Sabha elections and the assembly elections.

'Can you find out what is it that is holding Uddhav back? He has been cancelling on us. What is on his mind and what are his expectations? As you know, the chief ministership was not agreed upon,' he told GN.

GN got to work quickly and met Uddhav that very night at Matoshree. Uddhav told him, 'Fadnavis is not aware of these discussions (on chief ministership). The rotational chief ministership was absolutely discussed between Amitbhai and me. Also, I did not cancel the meeting, just pushed it by a few days. After Fadnavis had accused me of lying about the terms of sharing the chief ministership, it wouldn't be good optics for me to be meeting him immediately.'

GN asked, 'Can you remember when exactly Amitbhai made this commitment to you?'

Uddhav said, 'Yes, when he and I went into a separate room for a conversation on his visit to Matoshree before the Lok Sabha elections and also reiterated it while we drove to Blue Sea Banquets for the press conference to announce our alliance immediately after... Look, I understand that Fadnavis is not aware of my private discussions with Amitbhai. As long as he maintains the statement that he is unaware of these talks and does not accuse me of lying, I am okay with speaking to the BJP.'

After wrapping up the meeting, GN headed straight to Varsha to brief Fadnavis. It was very late at night, perhaps around 2 a.m. He said, 'Uddhav says Amitbhai made this commitment to him twice, on the phone and in a car... when they were on their way to the press conference in February.'

Fadnavis shot back, 'I can assure you that this has not happened. I was in the car when we went to the press conference. Perhaps Uddhav has forgotten that. And I am sure that this conversation did not take place.'

Fadnavis looked at GN and continued, 'You have been party to all the alliance talks, GN. After that meeting at your residence and the terms that followed, they still hold true. Even at your residence, when I spoke to Amitbhai over the phone late at night, he had clearly said that sharing the chief minister's post was out of the question. The only thing we have agreed on is to share posts and duties equally. We are happy to part with portfolios and important posts in the government with our allies.'

GN replied, 'I understand. Uddhav says the deal is on as long as you continue to maintain the position that you were not aware of what has been discussed between Amitbhai and Uddhav.'

Fadnavis concluded, 'It is okay for now, because it is partly true. However, there may be a time in the future when we may have to clarify that Amitbhai had not made any chief ministerial promise to the Sena. But, as of today, we'll keep that aside.'

30 October 2019, Matoshree

GN scheduled a meeting with Uddhav and reiterated what Fadnavis had discussed with him the previous night. He told Uddhav that the chief minister's post was not going to be up for discussion under any circumstances. He also told him that any other deal of equal power-sharing was possible. Uddhav, by then, had received indications from Sharad Pawar as well as the Congress that a Sena alliance with the NCP–Congress was no go.

Sensing that he may lose the opportunity to be a part of the government if the BJP too gave up courting him, he told GN, 'Fine. I would still want the deputy chief minister's post and an equal distribution in portfolios and important posts. Aaditya is the first Thackeray to contest an election and there is a demand from the party that he be made deputy chief minister.'

GN replied, 'That is something that sounds workable. Let me propose something here. If you can depute two leaders to sit with me, I can work out these details and take the proposal to Fadnavis.'

Uddhav consented and assigned Eknath Shinde and Subhash Desai to the job. For the next two days, the trio held extensive discussions at a five-star hotel in Mumbai's suburbs and arrived at the details of a workable solution for the Sena and the BJP. They decided on the allocation of portfolios and posts and after Uddhav had vetted it, GN said he would take the proposal to Fadnavis. It was agreed that Subhash Desai would join GN in the meeting with Fadnavis.

Sahyadri Guest House, Malabar Hill, Mumbai

The BJP held its first party legislature meet after the elections to choose the leader of the party's legislature. Fadnavis was re-elected to the post, unopposed. Addressing the elected BJP MLAs, he said, 'The mandate of the voters of Maharashtra is for the Mahayuti. Hence, the Mahayuti is going to soon form its government in the state.' He continued, 'Don't believe any rumours of any alternative formula that any other party may be working out. Just discount it as entertainment. We will form the government with the Shiv Sena soon. After 1995, no party in the state has been able to win more than 75 seats in the polls to the 288-member assembly, but the BJP managed to win 122 seats in 2014 and 105 in the recently concluded elections.'

To the party MLAs who had begun to question if they would be able to retain power, considering the tactics being adopted by the Sena, the confidence with which Fadnavis spoke proved to be a morale booster. Fadnavis was acutely aware that in situations like the one he now faced any sign of confusion could lead to defections and that really was the last thing he wanted at this point. Fadnavis's reiteration that the BJP would form government with the Sena was taken by certain sections of the media to be a sign of him softening his stance on the Sena's demands. However, he was quick to clarify that no offer of rotational chief ministership had been offered to the Sena as far as he knew.

While the BJP was electing its representatives, a similar exercise was being conducted by the NCP and the Congress as well, and the stage was being set for a final showdown. At the meeting of its MLAs, the NCP unanimously chose Ajit Pawar, who took back his resignation as the leader of their party legislature. 'Ajit Dada', as he is popularly known, reiterated to the media after the meet that the NCP would continue to do its job as an effective opposition party and point out flaws in the functioning of the government.

The Congress, on their part, elected Balasaheb Thorat who

also seemed quite prepared to take on the responsibility of a leader of the opposition party. The fact that the Congress was not only able to open its account by getting its leaders elected, but also perform decently, by winning 44 seats, was a redeeming factor for the party. It had performed miserably in the Lok Sabha polls at the Centre and had expected a similar show in the state elections. However, the Congress's strength in Maharashtra results from the iron hold that its firebrand leaders have on their individual constituencies. Despite having access to limited budgets to run effective campaigns, it was this hold and over 15 long years of service between 1999 and 2014 that made the victory of these 44 MLAs possible.

While addressing the press on the day of the assembly election, senior Congress leader Prithviraj Chavan had predicted that the results would lead to interesting possibilities, which would become clearer in 15 days. Now, speaking to the *Caravan* magazine, he said, 'The BJP has emerged as the single-largest party in the state assembly polls. If the BJP fails to form the government in the state, the Shiv Sena, being the second-largest party, will get an opportunity to form the government. Fadnavis had a very strong government in the last five years. He will not be as strong [again] even if he becomes the chief minister. There is a question mark on that because the Shiv Sena has been asking for the chief ministership for a very long time. They have the numbers to stop Fadnavis from occupying the chair.

'It is not a straightforward situation where Fadnavis just goes out and takes oath [as the] chief minister, like in 2014. It is a far more complicated situation. One cannot rule out the possibility of the Shiv Sena deciding to sit in the Opposition. The proposal of allying with us and the NCP has to come from the Shiv Sena. If at all that proposal comes, we will discuss it with our alliance partner, NCP, and other friendly parties. And, of course, the Congress would like to seek concurrence from the national leadership.'[9]

Again, later, in January 2020, he revealed in an interview to the Press Trust of India that in 2014 the Shiv Sena had approached the Congress to form a government in Maharashtra. Since he was at the helm of affairs as the chief minister then, he had taken the proposal to Sonia Gandhi who had rejected it.[10] Many reliable insiders in high positions have echoed Prithviraj Chavan's position and revealed that the talks between the Shiv Sena, the NCP and the Congress about forming a tripartite government in Maharashtra had been going on for a long time and had picked up steam before the Lok Sabha elections of 2019.

6

THE SENA SWITCHES SIDES

The tenure of the previous legislative assembly was to end on 8 November. While the Shiv Sena continued to do the rounds of Silver Oak, soliciting support, the top leaders of the BJP continued to huddle together and engage in core committee meetings as they maintained a wait-and-watch approach. If the term of the legislative assembly ended with no government in sight, several constitutional options would get activated and the role of the state's Governor would become important.

31 October 2019

The posters demanding that Aaditya Thackeray be made the next chief minister of Maharashtra were taken down from Dadar and other areas of Mumbai just as abruptly as they had been put up.[1]

Later in the day, Sanjay Raut spoke to select media persons outside the Sena Bhavan. 'I met Sharad Pawar at his residence today. See, the NCP and the Congress MLAs have been sending us feelers. The BJP is delaying the government formation by not fulfilling the power-sharing promise that they made to us. The delay in government formation is from the BJP's side. The political situation in Maharashtra is such that all political parties are speaking to each other except the BJP and the Sena. Our alliance has the public mandate, so we must come together and find a solution.'

A couple of hours later, Sharad Pawar too was seen speaking to the media. He had just finished a meeting with senior leaders of the NCP – Ajit Pawar, Chhagan Bhujbal, Dhananjay Munde, Jayant Patil and several others. He said, 'No, I have not met Sanjay Raut today. The NCP has no role to play in the government formation of the state. The Shiv Sena and the BJP have got the people's mandate.'

The two contradictory statements left observers wondering who lied that day.

Was it Raut? Had he said what he did to mount more pressure on the BJP to agree to the rotational chief ministerial arrangement? It was also noticed that this was perhaps the only time when Raut or any other Shiv Sena representative had said anything favourable about the Mahayuti.

Or was it Pawar who had made a false statement in order to indicate that he was not committed to the Sena as yet and to keep the Sena, the Congress as well as the BJP on tenterhooks and extract the best possible deal from them?

1 November 2019, Varsha

The BJP core committee met at the chief minister's residence to discuss the growing friendship between the Shiv Sena and the NCP.

'What are our options, sir?' one of them asked Fadnavis, as the others looked on expectantly, worry written on their brows.

'Look, there is no possibility as of now of conceding the chief minister's post to them. They don't have numbers equal to ours and shouldn't be diluting the importance of the post,' Fadnavis said.

'Sir, they are making a joke out of our alliance. They're exploring all sorts of options and alliances. Pawar Saheb [Sharad Pawar] seems to be taking an active role in fuelling the Sena's dissent,' said another.

'Let them evaluate and explore. We must sit quietly and adopt a wait-and-watch approach. We all know that this is a double-edged sword for the Sena. If they are to ally with us, they have to accept that their numbers are lower and they will be the junior partner in the alliance. If they ally with the others, they will have to dilute the very ideology that their party is built on.'

'Sir, they have not been answering our calls or returning them. We are in a complete communication lockdown with the Sena. And Sanjay Raut has been blaming us for not communicating with them.'

Fadnavis said, 'Let us leave media tactics out of this. Our interlocutor is doing his job. From the looks of it, the NCP and the Congress are not very keen on offering their support to the Sena.'

The meeting was adjourned, and as the leaders emerged the waiting media threw innumerable questions at them.

Sudhir Mungantiwar, a senior leader of the BJP and minister

of finance in the Fadnavis Cabinet, who is usually media shy, told the waiting reporters, 'The Sena's demand for the chief minister's post is the main hurdle in forming government at this point. As you all know, our tenure ends on 8 November. A new government will have to be in place within the stipulated time, or else the President will have to intervene. President's Rule will be imposed if the government is not formed within the given time.'

A reporter asked him, 'Mungantiwarji, Sanjay Raut has said that it is because the BJP isn't willing to fulfil its promise to the Sena that there is a delay in government formation. What are your thoughts on his statement?'

Mungantiwar shot back, 'Just like the BJP, the Sena also wants the government to be formed at the earliest. We fought the election as an alliance. The issue here is not of the Sena or the BJP, but the people of Maharashtra. If there is a deadlock, the BJP will make all efforts at the state level to make the first move and resolve the deadlock. If need be, our party's central leadership will also intervene.'

Another reporter queried, 'Will the BJP concede to the Shiv Sena's demand for the chief minister's post?'

'Certainly not, we have already named Devendra Fadnavis as our chief minister,'[2] replied Mungantiwar.

Later That Night, Varsha

GN and Subhash Desai arrived at Fadnavis's residence. They showed him the proposal that they had worked out. Fadnavis took a quick look at it and said, 'This looks workable. I'll show it to Amitbhai before I make any formal commitments, but I don't suspect there'll be any major issues.'

GN asked Fadnavis, 'Could you call Uddhavji and let him know that this proposal seems okay to you?'

Fadnavis replied, 'Yes, of course. Please advise a suitable time for the call.'

Desai quickly checked his phone and said, '11.30 a.m. tomorrow works fine for him.'

Fadnavis replied, 'Perfect. I shall call Uddhavji then. Thank you.'

2 November, 11.30 a.m., Varsha

Fadnavis called Uddhav at the pre-decided time. However, Uddhav's phone was busy. Fadnavis therefore sent a text message to Milind Narvekar informing him that he had been trying to reach Uddhav. Milind replied saying that Uddhav was on the other line and would return his call shortly.

On the phone, Uddhav was speaking with Ashok Chavan who was informing Uddhav that Sonia Gandhi, fearing a split in the Congress, was warming up to the idea of offering support to a Sena-led government. This was music to Uddhav's ears.

When 15 minutes had passed since Milind's reply, Fadnavis called Uddhav on his mobile phone once again. Uddhav, it seemed, was still busy on the other line and didn't take Fadnavis's call.

Immediately, Fadnavis's phone beeped signalling a message had arrived. It was from Milind. 'Sir,' it said, 'I am really sorry, but Uddhavji is still on the other line.'

Fadnavis waited. Another 15 minutes passed and there was no call from Uddhav. He once again picked up the phone and rang Uddhav. The call went unanswered. So he sent Milind a strongly worded text message expressing his displeasure.

Milind replied with an apology, 'I am really sorry. It seems like Uddhavji has changed his mind about allying with the BJP.'

That message marked the end of the road for the Mahayuti.

The day had started with *Saamna* carrying an editorial written by Sanjay Raut titled, 'Insult to Maharashtra. Is the President of India in your pocket?' The editorial asked if the President of India's seal was lying in the BJP's office in Maharashtra – why else would the party leaders be invoking his name? It went on to say, 'The President is the supreme authority in the Constitution. It is not about the individual, but the country. The country is not in anybody's pocket.'[3]

It was clear that the editorial was referring to Mungantiwar's statements citing President's Rule in the state. What was also clear was that Raut's statements had nothing to do with reality; they were aimed to instigate. Mungantiwar had at no point made a personal reference to the President of India. He had merely cited a possibility, listed in the Constitution of India, that if a government has not been formed by the time the tenure of the legislative assembly ends, the President has to intervene. Raut, it seems, was not aware that while the executive power of the Union does vest with the President (under Article 53 of the Constitution of India), he is required to exercise this power only in accordance with the advice of the council of ministers headed by the prime minister (Article 74). Whether Raut made the statement with an intent to misinform the limited readership of *Saamna* is a matter of opinion. But, knowing fully well that the old Sena was almost a militant outfit, he should have been cognizant of the fact that provocative statements of this nature could charge up the cadre.

In an interview on 1 November, Sharad Pawar had vehemently denied that his party was joining hands with the Sena and had stressed that the people's mandate was for the NCP to sit in the opposition benches. On 2 November, Nawab Malik, spokesperson for the NCP, tweeted, 'The NCP will definitely take a positive view if the Shiv Sena is ready to form the people's government as envisaged by Chhatrapati Shivaji Maharaj, minus the BJP. The alternative will be available if any decision is taken in the interest of the people to form a government.'[4]

3 November 2019, Varsha

TS (name changed to maintain confidentiality), a former Cabinet minister during the NCP–Congress regime in Maharashtra, and MD (name changed to maintain confidentiality), a current minister in the Thackeray Cabinet – both leaders of the top rung of the NCP – walked into Fadnavis's home, carefully avoiding drawing attention to themselves.

They were escorted briskly into Fadnavis's home office. After a few minutes of small talk, TS pitched to him, 'Devendraji we have come here as emissaries of Sharad Pawar Saheb. He has asked us to convey to you that the NCP would be happy to support the BJP in forming the government in Maharashtra, now that talks between you and the Sena have stalled.'

Fadnavis replied, 'Hmm. I have to involve Amitbhai in this discussion. Let me talk to him and we will see what to do. I will loop you in once I have more details.'

After the duo from the NCP left, Fadnavis informed Amit Shah about Sharad Pawar's proposal. The matter being extremely time sensitive, Amit Shah scheduled a meeting with the top brass of both parties the very next day at his residence in New Delhi.

4 November 2019, Amit Shah's Residence, New Delhi

Fadnavis reached Amit Shah's residence a little before the scheduled meeting with the NCP leaders. He wanted to loop Shah into the latest developments and discuss the strategy ahead. He also wanted to seek additional funds from the Centre to assist the farmers whose crops were damaged due to unseasonal rains.

At the scheduled time, Sharad Pawar, Ajit Pawar and PR (name changed), a former Union minister from the NCP, then in the UPA government, arrived at Shah's residence. They were escorted into the room where the five men held discussions regarding a possible post-poll alliance. It made sense. The numbers would be enough to form a stable government in the state.

Pawar confirmed to Shah his intention of supporting the BJP. After much deliberation over the terms of the deal, Shah gave his consent to take the talks forward with them.

One important concern they discussed was how to make the announcement of the parties coming together. They were, after all, on ideologically diverse paths. Sharad Pawar suggested, 'We will ensure that our letter of support does not go out to any other party and we will decline to form government if and when the Governor invites us. Let President's Rule be imposed in the state. During the next two weeks, I will tour the state extensively. On returning to Mumbai, I will hold a press conference where I will announce that a stable government is required in Maharashtra and in order to provide a stable government, the NCP has decided to support the BJP in a post-poll alliance.'

Shah and Fadnavis agreed to the plan and the men shook hands, finalizing the deal.

For several days following this crucial meeting, Ajit Pawar and PR went to Varsha for back-to-back meetings to finalize portfolio allocations and distribution of important posts.

Later that Afternoon, 10 Janpath, New Delhi

Another interesting meeting took place on the same day at 10 Janpath, New Delhi. Sharad Pawar had been summoned by Sonia Gandhi for an update on the Maharashtra situation and to discuss her intent to support a potential alliance with the Sena. She needed Sharad Pawar to be in on the plan so that the numbers could cross the halfway mark of 144. However,

Pawar seemed non-committal. Perhaps the reason was that he had already finalized the deal with Amit Shah and Fadnavis. Speaking to the media waiting outside Sonia's residence, Sharad Pawar said, 'The Shiv Sena has taken a tough stand against the BJP. I will go to Mumbai and speak to my leaders. My party does not have the numbers to form the government. The BJP and the Shiv Sena will have the responsibility of forming the government first.'[5]

4 November 2019, Raj Bhavan

Sanjay Raut made his way to the Governor's residence. The instructions from Uddhav were clear. 'Please urge the Governor to invite the BJP, which is the single-largest party, to form the government. Only if they decline the Governor's invite will we have clarity and the opportunity as the second-largest party to do so.' Speaking to the media after leaving the Governor's residence, Raut said, 'Since there is confusion over the formation of government in Maharashtra, the Sena will not be an obstacle. I have urged the Governor to invite the party with the single-largest seat share, which is the BJP, to form the government.'[6]

This act of Raut urging the Governor to call upon the BJP to form government had several politically relevant connotations. The most important among these was that the Sena was confident that the Congress leadership was in favour of leaving the BJP in the cold. Whether the NCP, or even the Congress for that matter, would actually support the Shiv Sena should the Sena try to form the government was still to be seen. The Sena was banking on the fact that Sonia Gandhi would not only come around, but also eventually be able to convince Pawar to do the same. On the other hand, the BJP's failure to form the government, with the Sena and the NCP both unwilling to offer any support to it, would urge many independent MLAs and smaller parties to join the Sena fold, thus increasing its numbers and weakening the NDA.

7

CATCH-22

5 November 2019, Silver Oak

On 5 November, Sanjay Raut visited Sharad Pawar again at his Mumbai residence.

That Silver Oak had started getting so much attention from politicians was an interesting development. Sharad Pawar hadn't intended for it to ever be in the limelight. In fact, it is widely believed that before the ongoing political crisis, the last time he had held political meetings at his home was in 2012 when Ajit Pawar resigned as Maharashtra's deputy chief minister in the midst of the ₹70,000-crore scam in which he was accused of being involved. Silver Oak, a humble 3000 sq. ft bungalow in South Mumbai, houses Sharad Pawar and his wife, Pratibha *tai* Pawar, on the ground floor, and their daughter, Supriya Sule, her husband, Sadanand, and their two children on the first floor. The recent media attention that the home had started getting wasn't appreciated by the residents of the house and Supriya Sule had reportedly lashed out at the waiting cameramen, asking them to leave the family alone.[1]

Raut, in his trousers and classic bandhgala vest over his shirt, and sporting half-rimmed spectacles, settled on the couch on the ground floor living room, and Sharad Pawar joined him soon after. The patriarch didn't share his daughter's annoyance at the presence of the media. He looked calm, though his mind was working fast. All was progressing as per his plans and he wouldn't have it any other way, waiting cameramen included.

'*Bola*, Sanjay, how was your meeting with the Governor?' he asked.

Raut replied, 'I have urged him to invite the BJP to form the government. Sir, I am here to ask you on behalf of my boss… Can we expect your support?'

Pawar remained silent. Thinking. In a moment, he replied, 'Look, Raut, you guys and the BJP have been alliance partners for 25 years. You are bound to run in that direction. It is only natural. However, what I can commit to you is that the BJP will not be receiving my support.'

'But Pawar Saheb, that was not my question,' Raut said.

'I don't think I am in a position to say anything more to you, Raut,' Pawar said, ending the discussion.

As he left Silver Oak, Raut tried to keep a cheerful look intact on his face for the sake of the cameramen gathered outside, even though he didn't have clear answers to take back to Matoshree with him.

The situation as it stood now was a classic case of mutual mistrust. Sharad Pawar knew that if he supported the Sena this early on and gave it his word on forming the government, the Sena would take that offer, gift-wrap it with a fancy ribbon and take it to the BJP to negotiate a better bargain. He didn't want to be a chip in the game; he wanted to be the one making the rules for how it was to be played. On the other hand, the Sena didn't trust Sharad Pawar to keep his word of supporting it. They had seen Pawar offering outside support to the BJP in 2014 and he could very well repeat it this time as well.

But to get the chief minister's *kursi* or to be the true remote control to it, both parties, who clearly didn't have the numbers, needed each other. And they also needed the Congress.

Later that day, Sharad Pawar held a press conference where he said, 'I want to see how skilled Amit Shah is in connection with Maharashtra. The BJP has the numbers and they should form the government in the state. The NCP and the Congress don't have the numbers. If we did, we would have already formed the government by now. Our mandate is to sit in the opposition and we are happy doing that.'

A reported asked him, 'Pawar Saheb, is there a possibility of a Sena–NCP government?'

He replied, 'Where is the question of a Shiv Sena–NCP government? The BJP and the Sena have been together for the last 25 years; today or tomorrow, they will come together again.'[2]

Media reports later in the day indicated that Amit Shah had met Prime Minister Narendra Modi and senior BJP leader Bhupendra Yadav. The agenda was to discuss government formation in Maharashtra, but, as reported in the media, not much seemed to have changed on their front as the state's core committee wanted to stick to the 'wait-and-watch' approach.[3]

6 November 2019, Matoshree

A dozen or so Sainiks, most of them close to Uddhav, sat around the room talking in whispers. As Uddhav and Aaditya entered, an eerie silence fell over the room. This conversation was not going to be easy.

One of them started anyway. 'Saheb, there are some MLAs in the party who believe that the Sena must give up some of our demands and go along with the BJP in forming the government. They believe that they have been elected on this premise and any alternative associations will harm their political future.'

Uddhav asked, 'Is this just a small group or are most of our MLAs of this opinion?'

Another Sainik replied, 'Saheb, it seems like the party is equally divided in their opinion on this issue. There is a section that wants to see Aadityaji as the chief minister at all costs. On the other hand, there is another section, mostly comprising MLAs elected from rural constituencies who believe that they will not be able to give an answer to their people about a change in the ideological stand.'[4]

Once again, the room was enveloped in silence. No one wanted to address the elephant in the room. There was no way of saying how many seats the Sena had won because the BJP, as an ally, had not fielded their candidates from those seats. The common suspicion was that the number would be large. After all, it was on the plank of the common Hindutva ideology and the development activities in the last five years in the nation as well as the state that they had contested the Lok Sabha elections. Most of the MLAs had also talked about Article 370 extensively in their rallies, something for which the entire credit went to the BJP. Several of them even had Prime Minister Modi's pictures on their campaign banners.

What they also knew was that the BJP was aware of all of these things. Why would it concede the all-important chief ministership to a party that had won just a little more than half the number of seats that the BJP had won? It was an unreasonable ask. But the lure of power can be overwhelming. The thought that the Sena could overthrow the BJP if it wanted to, if Sharad Pawar willed it, egged Uddhav on.

Uddhav and Aaditya could not but take into cognizance that the right thing to do would be to admit that they had won just a little more than half the number of seats that the BJP had. This understanding in the truest sense would entail taking up the deal that the BJP was ready to make, one where Aaditya would get the deputy chief minister's position. With a little more bargaining, and if the BJP was particularly generous, they could even get a few more Cabinet portfolios. With this deal, they would be able to live up to the election promises made to their voters and remain true to Balasaheb's and their own ideology.

Their MLAs would also be satisfied to see a Thackeray in the deputy chief minister's post and there would be no threat of a split within the party. None of the MLAs expected the chief ministership, really. Precedent showed that since the time the alliance was conceived, the formula that was agreed upon was: '*Jiske aakde, uska CM*' (The one with the numbers gets to appoint the chief minister). The downside of this, of course, would be that they would have to continue playing second fiddle to the BJP and Fadnavis for at least another term.

But morality often finds no place in politics. It gets compromised for temporary gains – and that is what the next few days would witness.

8

NEW BEGINNINGS

7 November 2019
Morning, *Saamna* Office, Mumbai

The day's edition of *Saamna* carried an editorial that accused the BJP of indulging in horse-trading. It said that certain BJP MLAs who had been defeated in the election were distributing incentive 'packages' to newly elected MLAs from across parties to encourage them to cross over and join their party, regardless of their ideological affiliation.[1]

Evening, Matoshree

Sambhaji Bhide arrived at Matoshree at eight in the evening. The founder of Shiv Pratishthan Hindustan, 85-year-old Bhide is a right-wing mass leader closely associated with the RSS and the Hindutva ideology. Shiv Pratishthan Hindustan is a small organization as compared to the RSS, but it works on the same ideological principles. With a command over right-wing Maharashtrian youth, especially in rural areas, he is an important voice of experience in Maharashtra politics and his list of admirers includes Fadnavis, Uddhav as well as Prime Minister Narendra Modi.

Bhide had arrived at Matoshree hoping to talk to Uddhav, who had by now completely cut off communications with the BJP. The veteran had come with the intent of helping the parties break the stand-off. It seemed he was unaware of GN's failed attempt at intervention between the Sena and the BJP. However, Uddhav did not make himself available to meet Bhide, and Bhide was left red-faced. The message from Uddhav was clear – he was not in the mood to negotiate with either the BJP or any ideological mentor to his party.[2]

Nagpur, Maharashtra

Just a couple of days earlier, rumours were doing the rounds that Nitin Gadkari, BJP's heavyweight leader in Prime Minister Narendra Modi's Cabinet, was set to replace Fadnavis as the chief minister. Gadkari had shared a wonderful relationship with Balasaheb and back in the 1990s had often been a party to alliance discussions as a part of the BJP's core committee. In terms of stature in the party's infrastructure, his could be likened to that of the late Pramod Mahajan and Gopinath Munde. Gadkari had also been the leader of the Opposition when the NCP and the Congress had been in power in Maharshtra, which meant that he very familiar with Sharad Pawar and his brand of politics. His experience and knowledge of the workings of the alliance was what was required in this hour of crisis.

Gadkari even flew down to Maharashtra from Delhi on 7 November and there were reports that he would meet with Uddhav. His ears always on the ground, Gadkari sensed that Uddhav was firmly set on the demand of rotational chief ministership and that his stance stemmed from Congress–NCP support. Realizing that meeting Uddhav under the circumstances would yield no results, he decided against it.

Gadkari and Fadnavis both hail from Nagpur and their loyalists are known to be rivals. Knowing well that he needed to clear the air and dispel rumours that were hurting relationships within the party, Gadkari issued a statement on landing in Mumbai. He said, 'Devendra Fadnavis will be the chief minister. I am not going to come back to Maharashtra, leaving the Union Cabinet. As far as the alliance is concerned, as far as I know, no fifty-fifty power-sharing formula was agreed upon. If the alliance members want me to intervene, I will try my best to break the deadlock.'

Afternoon, Hotel Rangsharda, Dadar, Mumbai

After accusing the BJP of luring MLAs into its fold, the Shiv Sena, in an effort to protect its flock, moved all its MLAs to Hotel Rangsharda in Bandra.

Varsha

Ajit Pawar walked into Fadnavis's, residence for further talks on the details of their alliance. As they settled into the armchairs of the home office of the chief minister, Ajit Pawar said, 'Devendraji, although we have finalized everything from portfolio allocations to division of important posts, I am here to also finalize the guardian ministers.'

Fadnavis replied, 'Dada, we can even do this after staking claim and forming government, no?'

'We can but Pawar saheb insisted that I come to you and clarify beforehand,' said Ajit.

Fadnavis picked up the phone and dialled Sharad Pawar. Pawar on the line confirmed, 'Yes, I have sent Ajit to finalize the guardian minister allocation also with you because I don't want any tension between our parties later over this matter. Look, we want to strengthen our base in western Maharashtra, so we will require more of our leaders as guardian ministers in the Konkan belt.'

'Sure Pawarsaheb, that will not be a problem. I will draw up the details with Ajit Dada.'

After the phone call ended Fadnavis and Ajit Pawar finalized the allocations of the guardian ministries across Maharashtra as well.

8 November 2019

Late afternoon, Raj Bhavan, Maharashtra

The term of Maharashtra's previous legislative assembly had come to an end. Fadnavis tendered his resignation to Governor Bhagat Singh Koshyari after which he became the caretaker chief minister of Maharashtra. A caretaker chief minister and his government stay in office and continue to perform duties until a new chief minister and a regular government is elected or until the Governor dismisses them.

Evening, Sahyadri Guest House, Mumbai

Fadnavis, flanked by most of his Cabinet ministers, called a press conference. The expressionless and grim faces of the ministers gave away the tension in the room. Fadnavis had decided to break the silence that he had maintained so far on the deadlock with the Shiv Sena. He was angry that he could not form the government despite having received the people's mandate. He felt the people too were angry that despite their suffrage and the clear choice they'd made, the state was going through such uncertainty because the public servants they had elected to represent them could not agree on the leadership terms.

In an attempt to defuse some of the tension, Fadnavis started off with a joke. He said, 'Welcome everyone, I am here to give you good news today.' Those gathered in the room burst into laughter. Then he said with passion, 'We [the BJP and the Shiv Sena] fought together, and after the election Uddhav Thackeray at his press conference said that all options are open for them to form a government. This kind of mindset is not good for a party that has got elected on a mandate which was given to the Mahayuti alliance.'

He continued, 'We have never promised [the Sena] rotational chief ministership. There has been no discussion about giving the Sena two and a half years to rule, at least in my presence, and I was there through the entire meeting. I later asked the BJP president and Home Minister Amitbhai Shah and he has denied making any such promises... I have never said anything untoward against Uddhav Thackeray till date. I have tried to reach out to him multiple times after the results were announced. I have tried to talk to him on several occasions. I have called him on the phone, but he did not answer. The Shiv Sena consciously made sure that there was no communication with the BJP. However, at the same time, he was busy holding conversations with the Congress and the NCP thrice a day. This shows where his party's priorities lie.'

He went on to point out how some Sena leaders since the day of the election results had indulged in making slanderous statements. He said that the fact that the Sena had spoken ill about the prime minister of the country was shameful and not responsible politics. 'Given their statements, especially against the PM, we are stunned and hurt. No one from the BJP ever targeted Bal Thackeray or Uddhav Thackeray. The Sena has relentlessly attacked Modiji in a way that even our rivals haven't. We cannot accept it. It seems the Shiv Sena is not interested in continuing the alliance. This kind of language used by the Sena is unacceptable.'

Addressing the accusations made by other parties that the BJP was indulging in horse-trading, Fadnavis said, 'Give us proof instead of making baseless allegations. Let me tell you that there won't be another election and the BJP will only form a stable government – and we won't do it by horse-trading.'[3]

Later in the evening, Sena Bhavan, Mumbai

Almost as soon as Fadnavis's press conference ended, Uddhav called the media to the Sena Bhavan and held his own press meet. Here, the world saw an altogether different side of Uddhav – he no longer had his mild demeanour. It seemed the press conference had been called for the singular purpose of lambasting the BJP.

With Aaditya and other senior Sena leaders by his side, Uddhav, clad in a white kurta and looking grimmer than ever, started by saying, 'I just watched the outgoing chief minister's press conference and frankly I am worried for him. First of all, I would like to thank him because he said that the BJP and the Shiv Sena alliance has done great work for Maharashtra's development in the last five years. Whether we were in alliance or not, I can't say for sure, but I would like him to ask himself if the work that he boasts of could have been accomplished without us.

'I had committed to the BJP that we will work together for five years – because of which my party had never been a hurdle in any work done for the progress of Maharashtra. My father has taught me this lesson – before giving your word to someone, think about it tens and thousands of times; but after you have made a commitment, stand by it, come what may, at all costs. It is for this commitment to their word that the Shiv Sena is respected by the people.'

He continued, 'However, I am deeply saddened by one thing. This is probably the first time in the history of Maharashtra that the Shiv Sena, or the Thackeray *parivaar*, more specifically, I, the Shiv Sena's *pramukh*'s son, has been accused of lying. Maharashtra's people know very well how the Shiv Sena's *pramukh* was, how his son is, how the Thackeray *parivaar* is. With deep regret, I have to say that Devendra Fadnavis, with Amit Shah's support, has accused me of lying. I would like to tell Amit Shah and company that no matter how much you accuse me, the people know who is lying and who is telling the truth.

'Whatever was decided between us, only we are witness to. Before the Lok Sabha elections, I had not gone to Delhi; Amit Shah and Devendra Fadnavis had come to me. Even then, the alliance talks had faltered and I was the reason for that happening. When they had initially offered me the post of the deputy chief minister of Maharashtra, I told them that I am not so desperate that for the post of the deputy CM, I will keep the alliance intact. I said to them that I had made a promise to my father that one day I will induct a Shiv Sainik to the post of Maharashtra's chief minister. This promise I am definitely going to fulfil, and I don't need Devendra Fadnavis or Amit Shah's blessings to do so. Anyway, after communicating this, I got up and left.

'The next day after our discussions, Devendra called and asked, "*Kaay karaycha?* (What do you want to do?)" and I reiterated that I am firm on my word that I had given to my father; if you are okay with this arrangement, then you take a call.

'Amitbhai rang me up after that and asked me what I wanted. "*Uddhavji, kya chahte hai aap?* (What do you want?)"

I said to him too that I will stand by the promise I had made to my father.

'He said, "*Theek hai*, okay, whichever party wins more seats in the election, the chief minister will be theirs."

'I replied, "No, Amitbhai. Under this formula, we have been stabbing and stepping on each other for the past 25 years and eventually the middle ground we reach is never okay to both."

'So, he asked me again what I wanted. "*Phir kya chahte hai aap?* (Then, what do you want?)"

I said, "I want equal distribution of seats, equal power-sharing in government as well as two and a half years of rotational chief ministership."

'He replied to me, "*Theek hai, jab aapka CM rahega, aap humko consider karo. Jab humara rahega, tab hum aapko consider karenge.* (Okay, when your CM is there, you help us with approvals. When ours is there, we will help you.)"

'I thought that's fair. Once we have come together and formed a government, we must support each other. Soon after that discussion, Amitbhai came to Matoshree and we sat in the room that my father used to occupy... He said to me, "*Uddhavji, maine teh kiya hai ki mere samay mein humara rishta jo tha woh bigad gaya hai, isliye mein hi usse ab mere hi karyakal mein theek karna chahta hoon.* (I have decided that our relationship, which has turned sour during my term, I shall help to fix in my term itself.)"

'I said, "Amitbhai, whatever is decided between us, please inform your party." Devendra was then informed about it and he made a request to me: "Uddhavji, let's do one thing. If I am to tell my party at this stage that we have divided the time of the chief minister's term, it will not go down well with them and I'll have some issues within the party. So, let's keep this as an understanding between us for now."

'I now understand how that wordplay of his is being used against me. My demands of sharing *padh* (post) and *jawabdari* (responsibility) equally are being misinterpreted using wordplay. Isn't chief ministership a *padh* and a responsibility? Anyway, I don't need anyone's certificate to prove I am an honest man.

'I am proud of the Sainiks that in 2014 we stopped the BJP's Ashvamedha horse. And now we will stop the sweet-talking tactics that they're using to destroy us. It is interesting to see how people are driven crazy by power. Devendra is my friend, no – really – he is a great friend of mine. And just because he was the chief minister, I supported his party. If anyone else was in his place, I don't know if I would have lent my support. I really didn't expect this behaviour from him.

'The reason I stopped communicating with him is probably because of some of you media guys; precisely when he said to some of you that no power-sharing deal of this sort has been decided between us. If he had said, yes, this was decided but we are not in a position to grant this to the Sena, I could still understand. Whether I would accept that or not, would have been another decision. But saying that this agreement was not reached is a serious allegation and there is no way that I, Balasaheb's son, could face Maharashtra's *janata* as a liar. This statement coming from him was shocking and upsetting for me, which is why I cancelled the talks that were to be held between our parties.

'I would like to make it clear that I do not consider the BJP my enemy. I just think that they are lying and lying does not fit into the Shiv Sena's *parampara* (tradition).

'I have been more than accommodating with the BJP. Why are they even boasting about their strike rate? After winning the Lok Sabha elections, they had a clear idea of the constituencies where the alliance had won. They took most of those seats and gave us only 124, out of which many were those where our alliance had not won in the Lok Sabha elections. Chandrakant Patil himself has thanked us for accepting their needs and situation.

'Also, I want to clarify that I have never criticized the prime minister. In fact, Prime Minister Modi has called me his "younger brother" on two occasions and if this brotherhood has upset someone and made them spread misinformation, then I have nothing to say.

'Take another ally of theirs as an example. Dushyant Chautala, president of the Jannayak Janata Party (JJP), an NDA ally in Haryana, has openly said, "*Kya ab do Gujarati, jinke wahan lok fauj mein jaane se darte hai, humein sikhayenge?* (Will those two Gujaratis whose people fear joining the army teach us now?)." I have not made any such statements against Prime Minister Modi or Amitbhai.

'While cleaning up the Ganga, their hearts have gotten polluted with dirt. It is so unfortunate and I feel so bad today that I have been associating with the wrong people, those who can go to any extent for the sake of power.

'Devendra Fadnavis said in his press conference that he was shocked to hear me say on the day of the results that all options are open. Why is this shocking? You have been repeatedly saying that we will form the government, despite not having a clear majority. You haven't been communicating with us, the Sena, your alliance partner, and you also knew we were talking to the NCP and the Congress. So what methods were you going to use to come to power without our support? Reaching out to the NCP and the Congress is a political trick that I have learnt from the BJP's politics in other states.

'*Haan*, one more important point, Devendra said that I was too busy to talk to them and was talking to the NCP and the Congress three times in a day. How do you know? Are you keeping a watch on me? I did not talk to you not because I was busy, but because I did not want to talk to you. Anyway, there is no need to keep a watch on us, because whatever we do, we do out in the open. It's all out there. We are not doing anything behind anyone's back.

'To be honest, I am deeply saddened by the situation that has arisen because of the BJP. I urge them as the largest party to stake claim to form the government and use all their skills to get the numbers to form the government. All options are indeed open for everyone at this point.'[4]

Uddhav ended his press conference on that note. He spoke casually, mostly using the bullet points he had written down on a piece of paper and being prompted occasionally by the leaders accompanying him.

In the end, it became clear after the two media interactions of the day that the battle lines had been drawn between the parties and the war was in full swing.

The path ahead was now completely uncertain. In the event of the chief minister resigning, the decision-making powers passed on exclusively to the Governor.

As all parties expected the Governor to begin inviting them to stake claim, fears about party members being poached reached a peak. The Congress moved its MLAs to a luxury resort in Jaipur. Since Rajasthan is a Congress-ruled state under the chief ministership of Ashok Gehlot, security arrangements were taken care of easily and their MLAs kept safe from the prying eyes of the BJP. At much the same time, the NCP moved its MLAs to the Renaissance Mumbai Convention Centre Hotel in Powai, a suburb of Mumbai.

The Shiv Sena MLAs had so far been housed in Hotel Rangsharda. However, the facilities in the 30 rooms provided for them were inadequate; moreover, the hotel was right in the middle of Mumbai city, where all the action was taking place. The Sena therefore packed its MLAs into two AC buses and moved them to The Retreat Hotel and Convention Centre, an isolated beach property in Madh Island, Malad, on the outskirts of the city. The party also approached Mumbai's director general of police, Subodh Jaiswal, to amplify the security arrangements for their members. A letter to him written by Milind Narvekar said, 'Our legislators and associate members have been shifted from Hotel Rangsharda to The Retreat in Malad. They will be staying at the Malad hotel until 15 November. Since Shiv Sena President Uddhav Thackeray will be interacting with them frequently, we feel that adequate security should be provided to them.'[5]

9

GAMES GOVERNORS PLAY

9 November 2019

Raj Bhavan, Mumbai

Governor Bhagat Singh Koshyari is quintessentially an RSS man who took an active part in the protests against the Emergency between 1975 and 1977 and was imprisoned for his stand. A two-time MP, an MLA and a Member of the Legislative Council (MLC) from the BJP, Koshyari has also served as the chief minister of Uttarakhand from 2001 to 2002 and as the national vice president of the party. Although he keeps a low profile, Koshyari rose up the RSS ranks and mentored some of the prominent BJP leaders of today. His commitment to the RSS and years of dedication and service to the BJP was finally rewarded when he was appointed the Governor of Maharashtra in September 2019.

On the morning of 9 November 2019, the Governor summoned Fadnavis in his capacity as the acting chief minister and leader of his party's legislature and asked him to express the party's willingness and ability to form a government. As per Indian law, the single-largest party gets priority from the Governor to stake the claim to form government. If it is able to garner the required numbers, it then needs to prove its majority on the floor of the legislative assembly. A floor test is an instrument incorporated in the Constitution of India to ensure transparency in the democratic process. As a part of this procedure, the chief minister appointed by the Governor is asked to prove majority on the floor of the legislative assembly. If his party or alliance fails in the floor test, the chief minister has to resign.

The Governor gave Fadnavis a two-day deadline to stake his claim and prove his majority in the house.

The official statement from the Raj Bhavan in Mumbai read: 'Elections to the Maharashtra Legislative Assembly were held on October 21 and the results were declared on October 24. However, despite the passage of 15 days, no single party or alliance of parties has come forward to form government. The Governor has, therefore, decided to explore the possibility of formation of government and today asked the leader of the elected members of the single largest party, BJP, to convey its willingness and ability to form the government.'

10 November 2019

6 p.m., Raj Bhavan, Mumbai

BJP State President Chandrakant Patil and other BJP core committee leaders made their way to the Governor's residence and refused the Governor's offer to form the government in Maharashtra.

In a media interaction that immediately followed the refusal Chandrakant Patil said, 'We had a very good mandate, which is why the Governor has invited us to form the government. However, the Sena has not supported us in forming the government, even though the mandate is for the alliance government to be in power. We will not disregard it. If the Shiv Sena wants to insult the mandate given by the people and form a government with the Congress and the NCP, then our best wishes to them.'

In the wake of the BJP refusing to take up the Governor's offer and informing him of its decision a day earlier than the deadline, the next step to be taken by the Governor would be to immediately invite the second-largest party in terms of number of seats won – in this case the Shiv Sena. The Sena had not expected the BJP to turn down the Governor's invitation – that too a day earlier than the deadline – and it was now forced to spring into action earlier than planned. When the Governor had invited the BJP, it was clear that it would be unlikely for the latter to form government but its refusal to do so before the stipulated time meant that the window of political opportunity was further shortened for the other parties to work out the statistics. In fact, the other parties had prepared their teams for the eventuality that the BJP would take up the Governor's offer and stake their claim on forming the government. In a meeting of newly elected NCP legislators, for instance, Nawab Malik had made their stand clear. 'If the BJP stakes claim to form the government and the Shiv Sena votes against the BJP in the floor test to pull down the government, then we will think of supporting an alternative government led by the Shiv Sena,'[1] he had said.

8 p.m., Raj Bhavan, Mumbai

Once the BJP had refused his offer, later that evening, the Governor invited the Shiv Sena to form government. A team of Sena leaders, led by Eknath Shinde, visited the Raj Bhavan where the Governor asked them to convey their ability and willingness to form government and gave them 24 hours to do so.

The official statement from the Raj Bhavan this time around read: 'Yesterday, Devendra Fadnavis was called upon to express his willingness and ability to form government. However, today, he has shown unwillingness. The Governor has, therefore, asked the leader of the elected members of the second-largest party, the Shiv Sena, Shri Eknath Shinde, to convey its willingness and ability to form the government to him. The Sena will have to inform the Governor about its stand by Monday, 7.30 p.m.'

11 p.m., Matoshree

Later that night, Eknath Shinde, Anil Desai, Priyanka Chaturvedi, Milind Narvekar, Sanjay Raut and a few other Sena leaders were in a marathon three-hour meeting with Uddhav and Aaditya to chart out a twenty-four-hour strategy.[2]

'Uddhavji, there is consensus among the Congress legislators in Jaipur and their support will come through,' a leader present at the meeting said.

'But we need to obtain a letter of support from both parties, the NCP and the Congress. How do we expedite this?' Uddhav asked.

Milind offered, 'Sir, we don't have much time. Perhaps some of us can go to Delhi and connect you to Soniaji. I will talk to Ahmedbhai [Ahmed Patel] for the logistics.'

Uddhav said, 'Yes, we must not let go of this opportunity. We cannot afford a delay. This is our chance. Aaditya and I will meet Pawar Saheb tomorrow. Raut, can you set this up please?'

Raut said, 'Uddhavji, Pawar Saheb may be unwilling to come to Matoshree.'

'Then, we shall go to them. See if you can set up something halfway. Milind and Anilji, make your travel arrangements and leave first thing in the morning. Keep me updated. Aaditya, you will go to the Governor tomorrow evening along with Shindeji to stake claim. Meanwhile, we must ensure that our legislators are safe from prying eyes. Be absolutely alert at The Retreat and watch out for any funny business. Aaditya, please stay there tonight,' Uddhav instructed.

Aaditya replied, 'I will make my way to the hotel right away.'

He reached The Retreat a few hours after midnight and interacted with the MLAs. He assured them that the Sena would stake a claim to form the government and were working on getting letters of support to this end from the NCP and the Congress.

Late at Night, Varsha

Fadnavis had just finished his day of meetings. It had been an eventful day and BJP leaders were still going in and out of his residence while they all kept a close watch on the developments.

An alert for FaceTime audio sounded on his mobile phone, and Fadnavis took the call.

'Devendraji, *namashkar, mi* Ajit Pawar *bolto*. Hello Devendraji, this is Ajit Pawar speaking,' he heard from the other end.

Fadnavis was surprised to hear from Ajit Pawar at this time of night, that too on a day the BJP had expressed its inability to form the government. Besides when he had met Ajit Pawar just a couple of days earlier the latter had been privy to all the expedited discussions between the BJP and the NCP on government formation. Perhaps the call was about discussing the specifics on portfolios, Fadnavis thought, but he also knew that such things were best discussed in person. Whatever it was, Fadnavis needed to get Ajit Pawar's assurance that the NCP was going to stick to the discussed script and not lend its support to the Sena.

'*Bola, Dada*. Speak, Dada.'

'Devendraji, all the details between our parties have been worked out now and most of our cadre is in support of our party supporting the BJP.'

'The Sena still seems to be counting on the NCP's and the Congress's support. ' Fadnavis pointed out.

'Optics are different, Devendraji, you know that. Besides, this type of a three-party arrangement can never work.'

'So, you're not going to give your letter of support to the Sena tomorrow? Can I count on you?' asked Fadnavis.

'Yes, you can count on us. That letter will not come through. And in all probability, the Congress's letter will not come through either,' Ajit quipped.

'Is Pawar saheb of the same opinion?' Fadnavis asked.

'Yes, he is,' answered Ajit Pawar.

11 November 2019
Early Morning, Varsha

The BJP's core team had been huddled together to observe the political developments of the day. In the midst of the discussions, one of the leaders asked, 'Do you think we can rely on Sharad Pawar? He is clearly leading Uddhav on.'

Fadnavis thought about this and called Amit Shah. The duo decided that Sharad Pawar could not be trusted even if his letter of support for the Sena didn't come through that day. This particular move could just be eyewash and something else could be brewing behind the scenes.

'So, what do we do?' Fadnavis asked Amit Shah.

'The only way to ensure we can trust him, if at all, is if he is willing to give his word to the prime minister in person. Meanwhile, please inform the NCP leaders of the support we will need when they are invited by the Governor to form the government,' Amit Shah suggested.

'Yes, I agree,' said Fadnavis and ended the call.

11 November 2019
Morning, New Delhi

As one of the first significant developments of the day, the only Union Cabinet minister from the Shiv Sena, Arvind Sawant, resigned from his post of the minister of heavy industries. It was a clear indication from the Sena to Sharad Pawar and the Congress, both of whom had been mounting pressure on the party to exit the NDA in the Centre so that they could start serious talks about forming a tripartite government in Maharashtra.[3]

Meanwhile, Milind Narvekar and MP Anil Desai had made their way to New Delhi for their meeting with Ahmed Patel.

Several rounds of discussions had been carried out among the Congress leadership in Delhi and with the legislators housed in the Jaipur resort. There was consensus among the Maharashtra Congress leadership that they would support a Shiv Sena-led government and obstruct the BJP from returning to power. The out-in-the-open, frequent meetings between Raut and Sharad Pawar had built a perception among the NCP, the Congress and the Sena cadres that Sharad Pawar was ready to support the Sena. However, there were still a few who were sceptical about this.

In Maharashtra, Sanjay Nirupam, the Mumbai Congress chief who had been recently ousted from his post due to differences with the state party leadership, took to Twitter to say that the Congress supporting the Sena would be a mistake for the party. Even higher up, leaders like Mallikarjun Kharge and Sonia Gandhi herself believed that it would be a major ideological compromise to support the Sena and its radical Hindutva ideology. However, if the Congress dilly-dallied on their decision, the party also ran the risk of its legislators breaking ranks and moving to other parties in order to stay in positions of power.

As Ahmed Patel, Milind and Anil Desai sat down, the former informed them, 'Soniaji is almost convinced that in order to stop the split of the Maharashtra Congress she will have to offer support to a Sena-led government.'

Milind told him, 'But we will need your party's official letter of support, Ahmedbhai.'

Ahmed Patel replied that Sonia Gandhi would need to talk to Uddhav and he would arrange for this phone call. The trio then made its way to 10 Janpath from where Ahmed Patel called Uddhav on Milind's phone and handed the phone to Sonia. It was now 5 p.m.

After exchanging greetings, Uddhav thanked Sonia Gandhi for her support and urged her to provide his emissaries with an official letter of support.

'Uddhavji, we will keep our letter ready shortly and hand it over once I speak with Sharad Pawar,' said Sonia Gandhi.

She immediately instructed Ahmed Patel to prepare the letter and get Sharad Pawar on the line.

In a major round of meetings held earlier in the day, Sonia Gandhi had reluctantly agreed to support a Sena-led government. However, she was still unsure if she wanted to support it by becoming a part of the alliance or from the outside. She had called for a second round of meetings to decide on this. However, after her conversation with Uddhav, the pressure to make a decision increased and time was running out. She certainly didn't want to send a message to her party cadre that the Congress's top leadership had lost out on an opportunity due to an inability to make a timely decision.

Afternoon, Taj Lands End, Bandra

While Sonia Gandhi was grappling with making a crucial decision in Delhi, Uddhav and Aaditya were on their way to Taj Lands End in Bandra for a crucial meeting. Sharad Pawar's NCP was yet to officially announce its support to the Shiv Sena. They had held back on the pretext that the Congress was taking its time to make up its mind. Sharad Pawar had repeatedly said that NCP was partners with the Congress and they wouldn't make any decisions without taking their ally into confidence.

It is well known in political circles that Uddhav does not step out of Matoshree for meetings regardless of the seniority or political affiliations of the people he is to meet. However, his decision to meet Sharad Pawar and his team at a neutral venue conveyed the message that Uddhav was willing to let go of his ego and be flexible in order to accomplish his mission to form a Sena-led coalition. The meeting at Taj Lands End was seen to be one that would pave the way for the NCP to join the Sena's side.

Pawar was accompanied by his nephew and NCP legislative party leader, Ajit Pawar, and senior party leaders, Sunil Tatkare and Dilip Walse Patil. This was possibly the most important meeting in terms of its timing and the decision-makers who were involved – it had the potential to decide the course of Maharashtra's politics in the time to come.

Uddhav thanked Sharad Pawar for coming to the Taj. 'Saheb, from my leaders I understand that there may be some ideological concerns that you and Soniaji may have. I am here to tell you that we are open to holding discussions and reaching a mutually beneficial arrangement.'

Pawar said, 'Uddhavji, for a three-party coalition to be stable, we will need to arrive at a common minimum programme [CMP] that is acceptable to all parties. We have only two seats less than your party. Even our leaders will expect almost an equal power-sharing arrangement from you. We are also of the opinion that as long as you are still a part of the NDA, talks cannot progress. And then there is the issue of chief ministership. Aaditya is too young; senior leaders like Ajit Pawar and Ashok Chavan will not work under him. And the names that have been mentioned of other Sena leaders are not acceptable to us.'[4]

'We have to submit the letters of support today to the Governor, Pawar Saheb. We can work out the finer details of the alliance later,' Uddhav said.

'Uddhav, the time is just too little. I still have to talk to Soniaji. Whatever we decide will be a joint decision,' said Pawar.

'I just spoke to Soniaji on the phone right before coming here and formally requested her for her support. I understand your point, though. We will wait for further updates from you,' Uddhav replied.

As Uddhav drove home from the meeting with the Pawars, it became clear to him that Sonia Gandhi was delaying arriving at a decision because her party members needed to hold further consultations among themselves and with the NCP. Pawar, on his part, was not willing to make an official commitment until he had Sonia Gandhi's nod. Uddhav had already severed ties with the BJP and he now realized that for a Sena-led alternative government to work out he would really have to bend over backwards.

An hour after Sharad Pawar left the meeting at the Taj, he received a call from Sonia Gandhi's office.

When Sonia came on the line, she said, 'Sharadji, Uddhav has made a formal request for our support. Shall we send our letter of support?'

Sharad Pawar responded in a matter-of-fact manner, 'We have decided not to provide our letter of support today. We have almost the same number of seats as the Sena and a lot of issues still need to be resolved.'

Sonia ended the call and reprimanded Ahmed Patel and others for pushing her to offer her support so hurriedly. She was not one bit pleased with the fact that her party had its letter of support ready while Sharad Pawar remained non-committal.[5] Naturally, the question that arose was whether Sharad Pawar was playing both sides.

Amidst all the action, with the media repeatedly covering the meetings between the decision-makers in Delhi and Mumbai, many people had started to conclude that the NCP and the Congress would offer their formal support to the Sena that very day. The Uddhav–Sonia phone call had especially fuelled reports that the Sena had won the Congress's support. To clear the air, the Congress put out an evasive statement that said the party would send its leaders to Mumbai to hold further talks with the NCP.

Even as the day's events played out, the Governor's deadline loomed ahead.

7 p.m., Raj Bhavan, Mumbai

Aaditya Thackeray, accompanied by Eknath Shinde, Subhash Desai and a few other senior Sena leaders, went to Raj Bhavan with the intent of staking claim to form government. Since they were not able to submit letters of support from the NCP and the Congress, they asked the Governor for two days' time to acquire the letters. The Governor denied this request, saying that although they had shown the willingness to form government within the stipulated time frame, the lack of the support letters displayed their express inability to do so.

The official statement from the Raj Bhavan on denying the Sena the extra time they had requested for said, 'A delegation of leaders of the Shiv Sena met the Governor and expressed willingness to form government. However, they could not submit the requisite letters of support. Further, they submitted a letter requesting two days of extension of the deadline for submitting the letters of support. The Governor expressed his inability to give further extension.'

Soon after the Governor's refusal, Aaditya addressed the media that was waiting outside Raj Bhavan. Despite the setback, he put on a brave face. 'We have expressed our willingness to the Governor about forming a stable government in Maharashtra. We asked him for at least two days' time, but we weren't given the time. The claim to form a government wasn't denied, but the time was. We'll continue to put in efforts to form a government in the state. We are the second-largest party in the state and we have come here to express our willingness as was asked of us.'

He added, 'We have initiated talks with two parties. Both the parties have expressed their in-principle support to the Sena. They need a few extra days to complete their procedures, which is why we sought additional time from the Governor but he refused to grant it. However, we want to offer a stable government to Maharashtra and our efforts to form government will continue.'

9 p.m., Raj Bhavan, Mumbai

Less than an hour after Aaditya's press interaction, Ajit Pawar got a hurried phone call from the Governor's residence asking him to see the Governor within an hour. When he reached the Governor's residence, he was asked to prove his willingness and ability to form government in Maharashtra. He was given 24 hours to do so.

10

PRESIDENT'S RULE

12 November 2019

9.30 a.m., Lilavati Hospital, Mumbai

A few days earlier, Sanjay Raut had been admitted to Lilavati Hospital in Bandra after he had experienced chest pain. There, he had undergone angioplasty. The pressure of recent events had possibly taken a toll on his health. The morning after the Shiv Sena's failure to muster up the numbers, he tweeted:

> *'लहरों से डर कर नौका पार नहीं होती,*
> *कोशिश करने वालों की कभी हार नही होती।'*
> *बच्चन.*
> *हम होंगे कामयाब...*
> *जरूर होंगे...*

> ('One can't cross the waters if they fear the waves.
> Those who try, will never lose.' – Bachchan
> We will win. Surely, we will.)

Quoting the recital of a poem by actor Amitabh Bachchan, it was an expression of determination that Raut's party would succeed in its endeavours.

Raj Bhavan
11 a.m.

Way before the deadline was to lapse, the NCP sent a letter to Governor Koshyari seeking a 48-hour extension to furnish the required letters of support.

12 p.m.

Soon after receiving the NCP's letter, Governor Koshyari sent his report to the President of India recommending that President's Rule be imposed in Maharashtra. The interval between the NCP's letter asking for a time extension and the Governor report to the President was too short. Since the report was sent within an hour of the receipt of the NCP's letter, it seemed to observers that the draft report had been prepared earlier, in anticipation of the NCP declining to form government.

The official statement put out by Raj Bhavan read, 'The Governor of Maharashtra made a recommendation to the President that he made attempts to explore the possibility of formation of government by having appropriate communications with all the political parties who could have formed the government in alliance with other political parties. Unfortunately, his attempts to do so have failed so far. Keeping in view the situation, circumstances and ground realities, the Governor is satisfied that the situation has arisen in the State of Maharashtra in which it is impossible to constitute and/or form a stable government in the State.' His office also tweeted, 'He is satisfied that the government cannot be carried on in accordance with the Constitution and has today submitted a report as contemplated by provision of Article 356 of the Constitution.'[1]

The Prime Minister's Residence, New Delhi

For President's Rule to come into effect, approval from the prime minister and the Union Cabinet is a necessary requisite. Minutes before the prime minister was scheduled to leave for Brazil to attend the BRICS summit, the Union Cabinet assembled at his residence and approved a recommendation to the President to issue a proclamation under Article 356(1) of the Constitution imposing President's Rule in Maharashtra and keeping its legislative assembly under suspended animation.

The President of India, Ram Nath Kovind, who was attending a function in Sultanpur Lodhi in Punjab when the Governor sent in his report, returned to New Delhi that afternoon and signed the proclamation.

According to Article 356, the President may by a proclamation 'assume to himself all or any of the functions of the Government of the State and all or any of the powers vested in or exercisable by the Governor or anybody or [sic] authority in the State other than the legislature of the State'. The proclamation is effective for a maximum period of six months but can be revoked at any time.

5 p.m., Maharashtra

Following an excruciating 19 days in limbo, President's Rule was finally imposed in Maharashtra after the Union Cabinet's recommendation.

Yashwantrao Chavan Centre, Nariman Point, Mumbai

Earlier in the day, Congress leaders Mallikarjun Kharge, K.C. Venugopal and Ahmed Patel had flown down to Mumbai to hold talks with the leaders of the NCP and the Shiv Sena. Sharad Pawar, Ajit Pawar and other NCP leaders were engaged in discussions with them all afternoon in a room in the Yashwantrao Chavan Centre. When the news of President's Rule being imposed on the state broke in the media, it came as a shock to most of the people in the room, including the Sena leaders who were keeping a close watch on the meetings in progress.

Meanwhile, it gradually became clear that the NCP had not informed their partners about the letter they had sent to the Governor seeking an extension.

When they put two and two together, most people were of the opinion that the NCP's letter was the trigger behind the imposition of President's Rule in the state. The Congress and the Sena were suspicious about the timing of the letter. Had the NCP not sent the letter way before their deadline had lapsed, the Governor would not have sent his recommendations to the Centre and the Union Cabinet would not have been able to assemble in the nick of time, minutes before the prime minister was to fly to Brazil. A delay of just a few hours by the NCP in sending out the letter would have had a domino effect on how the events of the day would have played out. The imposition of President's Rule would have been impossible in the prime minister's absence and it would have given the tripartite coalition more time to produce proof that they would be able to form government in the state.

The Shiv Sena and the Congress grew closer after this incident and began to talk directly with each other, as both parties suspected that Sharad Pawar had triggered the unsavoury situation. Both parties accused him of engaging in delaying tactics in forming a three-party Sena-led government in the state.[2]

Late evening, Matoshree

During the course of the day, the Shiv Sena had sought the services of veteran Congress leader and lawyer Kapil Sibal and moved the Supreme Court of India against the Governor's refusal to grant them additional time to prove their ability to form government. However, the Supreme Court's registry asked the party to mention the matter on Wednesday at 10.30 in the morning as it would not be possible to form a bench on Tuesday night. As news of the imposition of President's Rule in Maharashtra broke out, the Sena also decided to file a second plea against the act.

In the petition, the Sena called the Governor's actions 'ex facie arbitrary and mala fide'. The petition stated that, Governor Koshyari gave 48 hours to the Bharatiya Janata

Party and just 24 hours to the Sena to get letters of support. It also said that this betrayed inherent mala fide intent against the petitioners as it sought to treat them differently and adversely compared to how the Governor reached out to the BJP. The Governor, the petition said, had acted in haste and his action of not giving the Shiv Sena two days to stake a claim was part of a well-concerted plan made by the BJP to invoke Article 356. The petition further stated, 'The Governor is duty bound to allow reasonable time for political parties to conclude their negotiations on government formation and not act as an agent mouthpiece of the central government.'

After President's Rule was imposed in the state, Uddhav called a press conference at Matoshree at 8 p.m. He was joined by Aaditya, who looked casual in a blue T-shirt, a stark contrast to his father, who appeared rather dishevelled. Uddhav narrated to the media the Shiv Sena's experience with the Governor over the previous two days. He reiterated, 'We met the honourable Governor yesterday and made a request to him that we would still like to stake claim for forming a government. We asked him for 48 hours to provide the required letters of support. In a state like Maharashtra, forming a stable government is no small task. Several matters need to be worked out.

'As you all already know, we were awaiting the letters of support from the NCP and the Congress. Unless matters between the three of us are worked out, it is unlikely that the letters of support will come through. Probably after many,

many years, Maharashtra has got a man as kind as Koshyari as Governor. I say this because when we requested him for 48 hours' time, he said why just 48 hours, I'll give you six months. So, now in these six months that we have been granted, the Sena along with the NCP and the Congress will sit together and work out a common minimum programme and take forward our claim to form the government.'

He further stated, 'The Shiv Sena and the BJP, having a similar ideology, have been in alliance for 25 years. But now, since the recent debacle, we have been trying to come together with the NCP and the Congress. Many people are asking how parties with such different ideologies can come together. First, I would like a clarification on how the BJP and Nitish Kumar can come together, how the BJP and Ram Vilas Paswan can come together, how the BJP and Mehbooba Mufti can come together. How have "*Modi hatao*" *bolne wale* (the ones who wanted to oust Modi) Chandrababu Naidu and the BJP come together? Despite their differences, they have still come together to form governments. I have asked for more information on this; once I receive it, we will study it and work out a plan for the three of us with different ideologies to come together.'

Late evening, Yashwantrao Chavan Centre

The Congress and the NCP leaders together addressed a joint press conference after the President's Rule was imposed. It was led by Sharad Pawar and Ahmed Patel. Both leaders criticized the Governor's decision. Ahmed Patel complained that the Congress had not even been invited to stake its claim on government formation.

Sharad Pawar clarified why he hadn't informed his prepoll ally, the Congress, before sending out the NCP's letter to the Governor asking for more time. He said it was an internal party decision and its members did not feel that keeping other parties in the know was a requirement.

Both of them stated that they would be holding further talks among themselves before initiating discussions with the Shiv Sena on the common minimum programme that Uddhav had brought up in his press interaction.

Now, it seemed that there was no rush to form a tripartite government. All the parties concerned had more than enough time to hold multiple discussions, bargain and extract the best possible deal.

The Shiv Sena seemed to be on the backfoot now – the President's Rule and the luxury of time it provided had sent the ball into Sharad Pawar's court. And Sharad Pawar was not a man to let go of an opportunity.

Later that night, Fadnavis thanked the NCP emissaries on the phone for their support in invoking the President's Rule in the state. All was going as per their pre-decided plan. He also sent out a message that Sharad Pawar must seek time from the prime minister for the final closure of their deal.

11

PAWAR POWER

13 November 2019
9 a.m., Lilavati Hospital, Mumbai

Another day, another tweet. This morning, Maharashtra woke up to another tweet from an ailing Sanjay Raut – yet again it quoted from an Amitabh Bachchan movie.

> *अग्नीपथ*
> *अग्नीपथ*
> *अग्नीपथ...*
>
> (*Agneepath*, *Agneepath*, *Agneepath*...)

Specifically, Raut's tweet referred to the Sena being aware that the road ahead was going to be tough and laden with challenges. After the previous day's developments, most political analysts were of the opinion that Sharad Pawar was hand in glove with the BJP and was just toying with the Shiv Sena.

To understand what an alliance between the Congress, the NCP and the Shiv Sena would entail one would have to step back a little in history.

Thus far the relations among the three had been a complex mix of rivalry and deep ties. On the one hand, most communication among the three had been strewn with insinuations and insults. If they formed an alliance, not only would they be required to forget these insults but they would also have to learn to coexist genially with one another. To anyone with a knowledge of their past relations this would seem to be a difficult task at best.

In the late 1990s when Sonia Gandhi entered politics, Balasaheb Thackeray had said that he would prefer handing power over to the British, who at least had the experience of ruling the country for 150 years.[1] As an answer to that, a senior Congress leader, Digvijay Singh, had called the Shiv Sena 'desi Taliban'.[2] Balasaheb had also said that during the years when the Congress was in power, 'India was reeling under the servitude of the Italian-born Sonia Gandhi' and that 'the Congress party leaders are a bunch of eunuchs ready to prostrate before Sonia'. The term 'eunuch' had later been used by Uddhav as well when referring to Congress leaders.[3] However, Uddhav possessed neither the power nor the attitude that Balasaheb had had; when compared to his father's statements, his seemed as light as feathers.

Balasaheb had not spared Sharad Pawar and the NCP either. Referring to Sharad Pawar in a television interview in 1999, when asked if there was a possibility his party would ally with the NCP, he had said, 'If politics is considered to be a game of scoundrels, it is for a man to decide whether he wants to be a gentleman or a scoundrel. If anyone wants to become a scoundrel, okay. But I will not go with a scoundrel, whoever he may be.'[4]

On the other hand, the NCP and the Shiv Sena also had old ties, especially personal ones. Sharad Pawar and Balasaheb Thackeray had been close for the most part of the time that they had known each other. In fact, in the 1960s, they had wanted to launch a magazine together, one that could compete with the likes of *Time* magazine. Their families were close too, which had led Balasaheb to concede an MP seat to Supriya Sule when she entered politics in 2006. In his autobiography, *On My Terms*, Sharad Pawar writes that despite being fierce rivals of the Shiv Sena, his wife, Pratibha, and he would often visit Matoshree for *gupshup*, or a chit-chat, and dinner when Balasaheb was alive.

The Shiv Sena and the Congress too had lingering ties. Balasaheb supported the Emergency during Prime Minister Indira Gandhi's tenure, albeit to escape arrest. He did not field any candidates in the Lok Sabha polls held in 1977, after the Emergency had been lifted. Balasaheb had also backed several Congress leaders for Bombay mayoral polls before the 1980s. It was only after Indira Gandhi's death in 1984 that the ties between the Shiv Sena and the Congress ended. The relationship had deteriorated after Rajiv Gandhi took over the Congress reins, followed by Sonia and Rahul Gandhi.

During the last two days of discussions, the NCP and the Congress came up with a draft of the CMP. This CMP they drafted was drawn from the alliance handbook of the United Progressive Alliance (UPA) and prescribed the policy going forward as well as ideological positions of the parties concerned. This CMP was meant to be the go-to document that would bind the tri-party alliance together but the Shiv Sena was given an opportunity to weigh in only after the other two parties had readied the draft.

The three parties then formed internal committees that would guide the negotiations regarding finalizing a stand on the CMP.

Sensing that Sharad Pawar was playing on both sides, the Congress leadership made every effort to justify to Sharad Pawar why a Sena-led tripartite government would be the way to go. Now that Sonia was supportive of such a government, they did not want to lose Sharad Pawar to the BJP. They convinced him that the NCP would get the best deal among the three parties and that if the NCP was to go ahead and support the BJP Sharad Pawar would not be able to work independently at all, given the strength of BJP's leadership in the state and in the centre.

Sharad Pawar appeared to give this some thought, but he knew too that he would need to continue to maintain his conversations with the BJP in order to extract the best possible deal from the evolving tripartite arrangement.

Undisclosed Suburban Five-Star Hotel, Mumbai

There were many reasons for the Congress and the Shiv Sena to think that Sharad Pawar was trying to delay the formation of the tripartite government. The most important one being the letter asking for an extension of the deadline that the NCP had sent to the Governor without consulting the other two parties. Another was the phone call between Sonia Gandhi and Sharad Pawar on 11 November when Pawar had informed her that the NCP would not be providing its letter of support to the Shiv Sena. Chastened by the stonewalling tactics of the NCP, Sonia Gandhi decided not to rely on Sharad Pawar's updates and deputed senior Congress leaders to iron out the details of the alliance. Responding to a request from the Congress for a one-on-one meeting, Uddhav met the Maharashtra Congress president, Balasaheb Thorat, senior Congress leader Manikrao Thakare and former chief minister of the state Ashok Chavan at an undisclosed suburban hotel to chart out a plan of action. At the meeting they also discussed Sharad Pawar's position to the extent they were aware and cleared all miscommunication.

16 November, Amit Shah's Residence, New Delhi

Amit Shah had accepted an interview request from the Asian News International (ANI). He had kept his silence until now, but had finally decided it was time to comment on the political developments in Maharashtra. When the interviewer asked him why the Governor had recommended President's Rule in the state before the NCP's deadline had ended, Amit Shah replied,

'Look, I have heard the Opposition's side of the story. The Governor, to my knowledge, has not bent any constitutional rules. The NCP sent the Governor a letter between 11.30 a.m. and 12 p.m. expressing its inability to form a government within the stipulated time. So, there was no requirement for the Governor to wait until 8.30 p.m. at all.'

The interviewer then said that there was criticism that the President's Rule was imposed in a hurry.

Amit Shah shot back, 'In no state has this much time been granted to form a government. All parties had 18 days to stake claim. Between the time the election results were announced and the time that the tenure of the Maharashtra legislative assembly ended there were 18 days. In those 18 days, there was no restriction on who could approach the Governor with a request to stake claim to form a government. If a party or an alliance had the majority, they could have approached the Governor at any time in those 18 days.

'The Governor's invitations started only after the legislature's term ended, which was on eighth November. In the 18 days before that, neither the Shiv Sena nor the Congress, nor the NCP approached the Governor. Even we, the BJP, were not able to establish a majority. So what could the Governor do? The Opposition criticizes that a particular party was given one day; another party was given two days, and so on. Now, the Governor has given all of us so much time. In this extended time, any party or cluster of parties is free to approach the honourable Governor any time to form a government as long as they can prove their majority.'

The interviewer then said, 'People say that the BJP has made a joke of the Constitution...'

Amit Shah replied, 'See, the Governor has given all the parties extended time now to form a government. The opposition parties are crying foul that they were not given enough time… I would like to ask them, why don't you, even today, go to the Governor with the numbers? Today is day five since the Shiv Sena was invited. If they had the numbers, they could have approached the Governor.'

The interviewer responded, 'But as the single largest party, aren't you going to even try to form a government?'

Amit Shah responded, 'Look, we fought [the elections] with our allies and contested on fewer seats than we did in 2014. From those seats, we won 105. With the ally, we could have comfortably formed a government. But our ally made a demand which was completely unacceptable to us. How could we try to form a government? In the event of our ally not supporting us, we have only 105 seats – these numbers are not enough to form a government.'

The interviewer then asked, 'You have formed a government with the PDP [People's Democratic Party] in Jammu and Kashmir, which has a completely different ideology than yours. Then what was the problem with making compromises with an ideologically similar party as the Shiv Sena?'

Amit Shah stated, '*Dekhiye*, it is not my party's culture to expose conversations which have taken place behind closed doors. We do not make these conversations public and it is not even right to do so. In multiple election rallies, myself, the prime minister and even Devendra Fadnavis for that matter have repeatedly said that if the Mahayuti comes back to power then Devendra Fadnavis will retain the chief minister's position. No one contradicted us then.

'After the elections, if there were fresh demands made that were completely unacceptable to us, what could we do? Invocation of President's Rule in Maharashtra is a loss only to the BJP. We have lost our caretaker chief minister and our caretaker government... What has the Opposition lost? By creating a high-octane campaign against President's Rule, they are trying to draw public sympathy, which is sad. They are underestimating the intelligence of the *janata*.

'All in all, I would like to conclude by saying to all those people who have been complaining about how the Governor did not give them a fair chance to form a government that even today you have the right to go to the Governor and form a government. You have the right, but you don't have the numbers. So, please don't go around playing victim and complaining that your democratic rights have been taken away.'

14 November 2019

Yashwantrao Chavan Centre

At the Yashwantrao Chavan Centre, the appointed committees of the Shiv Sena, the Congress and the NCP arrived at the final draft of the CMP. From the Shiv Sena's side, Eknath Shinde and Subhash Desai were present. Prithviraj Chavan, Ashok Chavan, Manikrao Thakare and Vijay Wadettiwar represented the Congress in the discussions. Sharad Pawar's trusted lieutenants, Jayant Patil, Nawab Malik and Chhagan Bhujbal represented the NCP. The objective was to not only finalize the draft of the CMP, but also to hold 'cordial, free and frank discussions' around government formation and sharing of crucial posts.

On emerging from the meeting, in a show of unity, Eknath Shinde, Prithviraj Chavan, Chhagan Bhujbal and Jayant Patil addressed the media jointly. 'We all met and discussed the common minimum programme. We have prepared our report. We will submit our draft to the party presidents of the respective parties. The party chiefs will discuss it and take a final call.'

When the NCP leaders went to report to Sharad Pawar that they might get the largest chunk of the bite and that the Sena was very compromising in their approach during the discussions, the patriarch began to warm up to the idea of being part of this three-party government. He was well aware that with the BJP in power at the Centre, remaining a part of the NDA certainly had several advantages. But, on the flip side, it would never give him the kind of power that leading a tripartite government would. And perhaps he could even execute a back-room deal for his daughter to get half the tenure of chief ministership.[5] Uddhav was open to sharing the chief minister's term and this made his joining forces with the Sena a much more interesting option. With Modi and Shah holding fort for the BJP at the Centre, Sharad Pawar knew that the real power now resided in the state. It had always been his unstated ambition to make her the first woman chief minister of Maharashtra. However, with Fadnavis helming the affairs in the state, there would be little room for his daughter Supriya to lead. He needed to pave the way for her by abandoning his formula of Ajit Pawar running the state and Supriya spending her energies at the Centre. Once the tripartite government was formed because of him, getting Supriya to become an MLA would not be difficult.[6]

He called the party members closest to him and informed them that he had changed his mind, and that supporting the Sena was the road he was going to take. The members protested, especially the young ones. They saw no future in a three-party patchy alliance, they said. But Sharad Pawar had made up his mind. There was no point in him thinking of a long-term plan when there were so many sweet benefits from a short-term compromise. But it was not time for him yet to inform the BJP. He decided he would wait.

Sahyadri Guest House, Mumbai

PR, one of the top leaders of the NCP who was also present at the meeting at Amit Shah's house along with Devendra Fadnavis, Sharad Pawar and Ajit Pawar earlier in the month, made his way to Fadnavis's office. He informed Fadnavis about Sharad Pawar's change of mind. He said, 'It is very unlikely at this point that Pawar Saheb will continue to support the BJP. He wants to leave a legacy... Due to his advanced age, this might be his last political stint.

'He really wants to clear his reputation and the way he can do that is to live up to his word given to his prepoll ally. The Congress is really keen on supporting a Sena-led government and just to prove that he is a man of his word, Pawar Saheb will support Uddhav. Besides, the Sena has inside information that the NCP is talking to you as well and they are really bending over backwards and giving all the power to Pawar saheb.'

'What is the opinion of the rest of the party leaders?' inquired Fadnavis.

'Devendraji, many MLAs will continue to support Pawar Saheb's decisions. The top brass of the party thinks he's making a mistake – that's all of us, barring Supriya *tai*. But he is in no mood to listen to any of us,' replied the NCP member.

After a pause, he said, 'There is one man who can still accomplish what you have set out to do and that's Ajit Dada. He is vehemently opposed to the idea of supporting a Sena-led coalition. He still has a decade or more left in active politics and strongly believes that this move may not only be detrimental to the party, but to his future prospects as well. Plus, as you know, there's also that angle of family politics where his son Parth is being sidelined and Rohit Pawar given encouragement. Then there's the cold war with Supriya *tai*, which just adds fuel to the fire. But, anyway, he is your man, Devendraji.'

'Can you communicate to him that we are open to speaking to him, even if he wishes to break party ranks – as long as he brings in the required numbers?' asked Fadnavis.

The NCP member replied, 'Yes, sir. I will keep you updated.'

Later in the day, Sahyadri Guest House, Mumbai

The BJP summoned all their elected MLAs to the Sahyadri Guest House in order to keep them informed about the new developments and the official party position amidst the confusion regarding government formation. The air buzzed with secret whispers among the 105 MLAs gathered there. The events of the past few days had surprised them, like they had most of the state.

As Chandrakant Patil took to the stage to address them, an uncharacteristic silence fell on the room. They all hoped that there was some good news, that Fadnavis and Amit Shah had worked out a new strategy to ensure that those who had won the election got their due.

In his usual composed, even tone, Chandrakant Patil began, 'The party is keeping a close watch on the ongoing political drama over the formation of the government in the state. If this unholy tripartite government is formed, it is certainly not going to last. It is against the people's mandate. The mandate is with us. We are the largest party in the state and we have the numbers to show for it. There are over 90,000 polling booths across Maharashtra and elections will be held in all these booths very soon again. From tomorrow, you all should visit the areas affected by the unseasonal rain and focus on helping the affected people. In short, prepare for re-elections.'

Fadnavis, as the leader of the BJP's party legislature, assured them that the people's mandate was with the BJP. Regardless of the political drama, it would be the BJP alone that would form the government, he said. He reiterated that there was no alternative to the BJP in Maharashtra. The MLAs cheered in excitement, seemingly re-energized by their party's fighting spirit.

15 November 2019
NCP Party Office, Churchgate, Mumbai

As instructed by Sharad Pawar, his PA rang the prime minister's office to set up an appointment. The PMO got back with a time on 20 November, five days later.

Meanwhile, reflecting Pawar's change in mood, the NCP spokesperson, Nawab Malik, held a press conference during which he questioned Chandrakant Patil's contention that the numbers showed that the BJP was the largest party in the state. He said, 'When they are saying they have the strength, why did they inform the Governor they will not be able to form a government? They do not have the adequate legislators; the reason they are making these statements is to stop their MLAs from running away. The BJP should understand that this is Maharashtra, not Goa or Karnataka [where the BJP formed governments despite having lower numbers than the Opposition parties].'

While the NCP, the Shiv Sena and the Congress held more rounds of talks, the seating of the Shiv Sena's MPs in the Union Parliament in New Delhi was changed to the opposition benches. They were officially considered to be out of the NDA.

17 November 2019, Silver Oak

The NCP's top leaders gathered at Sharad Pawar's residence. The next few days were going to be important, with Sharad Pawar scheduled to be in two back-to-back meetings. The first one was with Prime Minister Modi and the second one with Sonia Gandhi. Sharad Pawar needed one last word of assurance from his top men before going ahead with what he was about to do.

When he asked if they were happy to be a part of a non-BJP front led by the Sena, most of them gave neutral responses sensing that he had already made up his mind. There was only one man who vocally opposed it and continued to advocate supporting the BJP. This was Ajit Pawar. The other leaders were a little taken aback that Ajit Dada still hadn't fallen in line with Pawar Saheb's thoughts, but they left it to Pawar Saheb to convince his aggressive nephew.

On emerging from the meeting, Nawab Malik spoke to the media. He declared, 'After our party's core committee meeting, we have arrived at the conclusion that the President's Rule in Maharashtra should end and an alternative government should be formed. However, we have decided that the next steps will be taken only after a discussion with the Congress. Tomorrow, Congress president Sonia Gandhi and Pawar Saheb will hold a meeting in New Delhi, and day after tomorrow the leaders of the two parties will meet.'

Meanwhile, Raut, now back at his post and in good health, spoke to select media persons outside the Parliament in New Delhi, where he was attending the Rajya Sabha proceedings as an MP, and conveyed that the Shiv Sena had the support of 170 MLAs and that a Sena-led tripartite government would be formed by December 2019. He said, 'We will show the strength on the floor of the House. We will have the support of 170 MLAs. The Shiv Sena government in Maharashtra will run for five years and the support of the 170 MLAs will be seen in the Maharashtra assembly. Look, no one wants to form a government with the Bharatiya Janata Party. They have ditched the Shiv Sena; the people are no longer with the BJP. The discussions on the common minimum programme are ongoing and we are absolutely involved.'

He added, '*Agar kisi ko lagta hai ki Delhi unke baap ki hai, toh woh galat sochte hain. Aanewale dinon mein kya hone wala hai hamein pata hai.* (If some people think that Delhi belongs to their father, they have a misconception. We know what is going to happen in the coming days.)'

18 November 2019

Late morning, Parliament of India

On the day that the Rajya Sabha held its 250th session, Prime Minister Modi took to the floor. '*Main aaj do dalon ka ullekh karna chahta hoon. Ek hai NCP aur ek hai BJD* [*Biju Janata Dal*]. (I want to talk about two parties today, one is the NCP and the other the BJD.) Both the parties had decided that in spite of being in the Opposition, they will not come into the well to create havoc in the House. We all have something to learn from them, including my party. I have observed that not even once have they broken this rule they made for themselves. And it is to be noted that in spite of following this rule neither has the NCP's political progression suffered nor has the BJD's.'

The prime minister's praise at the time that a political

crisis was brewing in Maharashtra raised many eyebrows. Many believed that it was just the nudge required to deter Sharad Pawar from supporting the Sena. Many also began to wonder if Sharad Pawar and the BJP, particularly the Prime Minister were growing closer, way more than the media or the observers could see, despite his intent to support the Sena-led government.

Late afternoon, 10 Janpath, New Delhi

There was a meeting between Sonia Gandhi and Sharad Pawar after the Parliament's proceedings had adjourned for the day. Clad in his usual white safari suit, Sharad Pawar made his way to 10 Janpath. He kept his gaze steady as he observed media persons around Sonia Gandhi's house following his every movement. He was truly the man of the hour. He was the one who could enable or disable the various political parties' efforts to form a new government in Maharashtra. Some people had begun to call him the Chanakya of Maharashtra and who would not enjoy that title!

Sharad Pawar settled into the meeting with Sonia Gandhi and A.K. Antony, former defence minister and a true-blue Congress man. He informed them, 'I do think Soniaji that now my party is ready to support this alliance. I understand that there have been some concerns from the Congress's side on the CM's post being given to a Thackeray. Uddhav is really the only man who commands enough respect from all the three parties to be able to manage this delicate association.'

Sonia and Antony voiced their opinions on how Balasaheb

and the Gandhis had an extremely strained relationship and now supporting a Thackeray chief minister would just not make sense to the polity. At that point, Pawar had to go into the history of the Thackeray–Gandhi relationship and remind them that Balasaheb had been very supportive of Indira Gandhi back in the 1970s. He came up with a few anecdotes to illustrate the cordial nature of their relationship and was thus able to win Sonia Gandhi's confidence on giving the chief minister's post to Uddhav. Moreover, she was happy that Sharad Pawar was living up to his prepoll pact with the Congress and hadn't ditched them for the BJP. The three leaders worked out the plan of action to be followed in the next few days and also some details on portfolio distribution. Once the meeting concluded, they seemed to be confident about staking a claim to form government in Maharashtra the following week.

Now that this meeting was out of the way, Sharad Pawar had to manage his scheduled meeting with Prime Minister Modi two days later. It wasn't in Sharad Pawar's nature to break relationships, specially one with the Prime Minister of India. After all, he had friends across party lines.

By the time he exited 10 Janpath, more cameramen and reporters had gathered. For Sharad Pawar, it was too early to reveal his plans of supporting the Sena to the people, to the BJP and also, to some extent, to the Sena. A lot more bargaining had to happen in the tri-party discussions and if he gave away his true intent, he would lose his bargaining power. To the waiting media he said, 'I just had a meeting with the Congress president. A.K. Antony was also present. We discussed in detail Maharashtra's political situation. I have briefed her about the situation. However, no discussion on government formation took place. We only discussed the current situation and the numbers. Today's meeting was merely a briefing.'

A curious reporter asked, 'Are you open to supporting a Sena-led government?'

With a glint of mischief in his eyes, Sharad Pawar replied, 'The Shiv Sena and the BJP have been allies for a long time. They have contested the election together as allies, as have the Congress and the NCP. They have to choose their path ahead and then we will do our politics. *Woh apni rajneeti karenge, aur hum apni.* (They will do their politics, we will do ours.) After the media reports and rumours about the NCP and the Congress, several of our colleagues were upset that we were not keeping them in the know. The Swabhimani Shetkari Sangathana was our ally in the election. Their MLA won. We can't ignore them. We had given some seats to the Samajwadi Party as well. Their MLAs have also won. The Peasants and Workers Party had also been given some seats. They didn't win, but they are still our allies. The Republican group too supported us. We have to take them all into confidence should we decide to go with a particular party. No discussions of this nature have taken place yet.'

More persistence from reporters followed. 'Pawar Saheb, Sanjay Raut has claimed that the Shiv Sena has support from 170 MLAs, implying that the NCP and the Congress are supporting them...'

Even before the reporter could complete the question, Pawar said, 'You should ask Sanjay Raut about these numbers and how a responsible Member of Parliament like him can make such claims. We have not made any such commitment to him. In today's meeting, we have decided that the senior leaders of both the NCP and the Congress will meet. We will take everyone's point of view and take them into confidence and then together decide a further course of action.'

He was slightly irked at a female journalist who asked him about an independent MLA in Maharashtra who had said that the NCP was likely to support the BJP. He replied, looking perturbed, 'Ah, so you think an independent MLA will decide what my party is supposed to do?' Before anyone could ask any further questions, he reiterated, 'Today, we only discussed our own parties. No other parties were discussed.'

Sharad Pawar thus bowled a googly in Delhi leaving many hopefuls from the Sena quite dejected. Power was so close at hand and yet Sharad Pawar was proving to be unreliable. The Sainiks believed they had entrusted enough power in his hands to lure him. Perhaps, they were wrong. Perhaps, Sharad Pawar could not be lured. Or, even worse, perhaps the BJP was offering him a better deal?

Afternoon, Varsha

Devendra Fadnavis sent a cryptic message to Ajit Pawar over the phone: 'Dada, looks like Pawar Saheb is backing out of the BJP–NCP deal. All our informants have indicated so. What is going on?'

Ajit Pawar replied, 'This is true. He thinks he will be able to have his cake and eat it too, if he supports the Sena. All the power will be in his hands. And who would turn down an opportunity like that?'

'Where do you stand?' asked Fadnavis.

'Still with the BJP and you,' responded Ajit Pawar.

'Can you get enough numbers so that we can form a majority government together?' inquired Fadnavis.

'There are about 28 MLAs already who are on my side and who will do what I say. With your numbers and the independents, we should be close to the halfway mark,' replied Ajit Pawar.

'Who are they?' asked Fadnavis.

'Sunil Shelke, Sandeep Kshirsagar, Rajendra Shingne, Sunil Bhusara, Manikrao Kokate, Dilip Bankar, Sunil Tingre, Dhananjay Munde, Prakash Solanke, Sanjay Bansode, Narhari Jhirval, Babasaheb Patil, Daulat Daroda, Nitin Pawar, Anil Patil, plus 13 more' Ajit Pawar reeled out the names confidently.[7]

'Do you want to shift them out of the state so that they can remain safe?' asked Fadnavis.

'*Nahi, nahi. Ithech thambu dya.* No, no. Let them stay here. If they stay with the rest of the flock, perhaps they can convert a few more. I will strategize with these confidants of mine and we'll form groups of four MLAs from the NCP cadre. Each of my 28 confidants will act as a group leader. Each group leader will be given the responsibility to convert at least one one or two other MLA to our side,' Ajit Pawar said.

'Hmm… This has to be foolproof, Dada. You know what a big risk we will be taking, right?' Fadnavis sounded uncertain.

'Don't worry, Devendraji. I will put you in touch with all of these group leaders so that you are well in the loop,' Ajit Pawar assured him.

Fadnavis seemed satisfied with Ajit Pawar's solution. But he knew he would feel more comfortable once he spoke to Ajit's chosen men. He immediately rang up Amit Shah and informed him of the details of his discussions with Ajit Pawar. Amit Shah seemed convinced, but he also stressed on Fadnavis being in touch with the group within the NCP cadre so that there was no room for doubt.

19 November 2019, 10 Janpath, New Delhi

Sonia Gandhi and Sharad Pawar chaired a meeting with senior Congress and NCP leaders. Many of them had flown to Delhi from Maharashtra overnight to participate in this meeting. The main agenda was to discuss and decide amongst themselves what each party should demand and expect from the Sena should a three-party alliance be formed. Both parties needed to be on the same page to hold further talks with the Sainiks and they needed to be well aware of each other's expectations, leaving no room for any miscommunication. It was also important for them to come across as being as united as possible to extract the best possible bargain from the Sena.

Ajit Pawar appointed Dhananjay Munde as his representative for the parleys with Fadnavis.[8] Ajit Pawar himself could not continue to take calls from Fadnavis and his team since he was spending most of the time with his uncle in meetings one after the other. Dhananjay Munde is an upcoming dynamic leader of the NCP, and the nephew of the late Gopinath Munde, one-time star leader of the BJP. Dhananjay went rogue after Gopinath Munde's daughter was chosen to succeed the father. In Maharashtra, after the recent elections, he is also known as a 'giant killer' as he contested and won against Pankaja Munde, Gopinath's daughter and a core committee member of the state BJP unit.

20 November 2019, Parliament of India

Sharad Pawar's meeting with Prime Minister Modi was scheduled for late morning even as the winter proceedings of the Parliament were on. Just two days had passed since the NCP had received praise from the prime minister for its discipline and decorum. This meeting was going to be difficult. Pawar would have to convince the most powerful man in the country why he was backing out on his word and an agreed-upon deal. Sharad Pawar had wrapped a beige jacket over his trademark white safari suit, perhaps to elevate it to a slightly formal look for the occasion. He hurried into the meeting carrying a transparent envelope with documents in his left hand. Once he met the prime minister, the two men exchanged pleasantries before addressing the elephant in the room.

'Pawar Saheb, it would be nice if we are able to work together in Maharashtra,' said Modi, in his commanding, steady tone, completely aware of Pawar's commitments made to the BJP.

'Modiji, you know we share a great relationship. But, unfortunately, political circumstances will not permit me to work with your party this time. I will be forming a government with the Congress and the Shiv Sena,' answered Pawar, not one bit intimidated.

'I see. In that case, I wish you good luck.'

When Sharad Pawar emerged from the meeting an hour later, he told the media that he had met with the prime minister to discuss the aid needed from the Centre for distressed farmers in Maharashtra.

Back in Maharashtra, the long meeting between Sharad Pawar and the prime minister at such a critical political juncture did not go down well with the Shiv Sena and the Congress. Both parties got extremely nervous and began to once again doubt Sharad Pawar's loyalties.

In an interview given by Sharad Pawar to ABP Majha much later, on 3 December, he mentioned that the prime minister had offered his daughter Supriya Sule a Cabinet berth at the Centre in exchange of the NCP's support to the BJP. However, Fadnavis was quick to counter these claims as false. He said, 'Pawar is not revealing all the details about the meeting with the prime minister. There are so many things that are not yet known which the PM will reveal at the right time.'[9]

Immediately after the Pawar–Modi meet, Sonia approved the alliance with the Shiv Sena on the condition that the Congress would withdraw if the Shiv Sena continued to adopt a communal agenda. Then the NCP and the Congress leaders in Maharashtra quickly summoned a press conference during which the questions were fielded by the NCP's Nawab Malik and the Congress's Prithviraj Chavan.

Prithviraj Chavan said, 'The Congress–NCP have had long and positive discussions over government formation in Maharashtra and discussions on this matter will continue for a few more days. The Congress–NCP will be able to give a stable government to Maharashtra in alliance with the Shiv Sena in the near future.'

Malik added, 'The Congress and the NCP have decided to provide an alternative government in Maharashtra and it can happen only when the NCP–Congress–Shiv Sena come together. The three parties are trying their best to resolve all issues and form a stable government in the state.'

21 November 2019, 10 Janpath, New Delhi

Top Congress leaders of Maharashtra like Ashok Chavan, Prithviraj Chavan and Balasaheb Thorat made their way to Sonia Gandhi's residence for a meeting of the Congress Working Committee. After Sonia had briefed them about her interaction with Sharad Pawar a few days ago, it was formally decided that the Congress would lend its support to the Sena-led alliance. They held extensive discussions on the terms of such a coalition and what Congress leaders should expect out of the deal.

Emerging from the meeting, Prithviraj Chavan briefed the media, 'Our ally, the NCP, and we have concluded almost all discussions on government formation in Maharashtra. There is complete unanimity between us. On the twenty-second of

November, we will have a meeting with our other alliance parties, and later in the day we will have discussions with the Shiv Sena. Then a decision will be taken on the structure of the alliance... When we announce the common minimum programme, the power-sharing formula will also be disclosed.'

Later in the Day, Twitter

Sanjay Raut posted another tweet, this time an emotionally charged, original one, but with its entertainment value intact: '*Kabhee kabhee kuchh rishton se baahar hee aa jaana achcha hota hai...ahankaar ke liye nahin, svaabhimaan ke liye.*' (Often, it is better to sever some relationships...not for the sake of pride, but for self-respect).

It was not difficult to figure out that Raut was bidding adieu to the BJP.

The day ended with yet another round of marathon meetings among the leaders of the Congress, the NCP and the Shiv Sena. Discussions on the chief minister's post too were had, where Sharad Pawar insisted that Uddhav be made the head of the government for a full five years. Uddhav was initially hesitant to accept this proposal and wanted another Sainik, particularly Aaditya, to assume the post. However, the NCP and the Congress believed that Uddhav's leadership was crucial to the stability of the alliance. He was the only one who could command power over the veteran leaders of all the three parties and keep the difficult ones in check.

During the meeting, they also discussed portfolios and how these could be allotted – who would be deputy chief minister, Speaker, etc., as well as what they would name the alliance. The Shiv Sena suggested the alliance be called Maha Shiv Aghadi. The Congress–NCP alliance was known as Maha Aghadi, the word '*aghadi*' meaning 'forward'. However, the Congress and the NCP objected to the word 'Shiv', derived as it was from the Shiv Sena's name. They insisted that none of the individual parties' names should be part of the alliance's name. After some thought, they collectively arrived at the name, Maha Vikas Aghadi ('*vikas*' meaning progress).

And so, by the end of the day on 21 November 2019, clarity had emerged that within a day or so, Maharashtra would have an Uddhav Thackeray-led tripartite government called Maha Vikas Aghadi.

22 November 2019, Nehru Centre, Worli, Mumbai

Nehru Centre, the iconic building at the heart of Mumbai, was chosen to close the government-formation discussions between the three parties.

All the participants knew the day was going to be a long one as many details were to be hammered out before the deadline they had announced for an official declaration. After all, the deadline was the end of that very day. After coming to a consensus, the parties would have to meet the Governor and stake claim to form a government, by showing both the willingness and the ability to do so.

Even as the discussions on portfolio distribution began, Ajit Pawar seemed to be in a foul mood. He demanded that the NCP have the lion's share of important portfolios. He followed up those demands with even more asks, which disturbed the discussions and stopped them from moving forward productively. He looked sweaty and restless throughout the meeting and appeared to be constantly busy on his phone, either texting or receiving calls, much to the annoyance of those present, who felt a lack of respect in his odd behaviour. Now, with the Sena and the Congress not agreeing on the new demands that Ajit Pawar continued to put forward, a heated argument broke out between the leaders who were already put off by his attitude.

After a while, Ajit Pawar got up, saying he had to take an important phone call and never returned to the meeting. He had left, not bothering to finish the debate. Without the NCP's legislative leader, the talks ended inconclusively.

His behaviour irritated Sharad Pawar too, though he kept a straight face while emerging from the building, fully aware that there would be media waiting outside. He announced that Uddhav Thackeray would be the leader of the tripartite alliance which would stake claim to form a government in the state very soon.[10]

Meanwhile, on leaving the meeting, Ajit Pawar called his trusted MLAs one by one. 'This deal with the Shiv Sena is a compromise. I am going to take a big step and I need you all by my side. Can I count on you?'[11]

12

A MIDNIGHT COUP

22 November 2019
1 p.m., Varsha

Ajit Pawar arrived at Varsha, immediately after he left the meeting at the Nehru Centre midway.

At Varsha, he told Fadnavis, 'Our talks at the Nehru Centre meeting were inconclusive today. I made some unreasonable demands which led to a heated debate, but I don't think we can stall them anymore. The MVA [Maha Vikas Aghadi] will be ready to stake their claim any moment now.'

Fadnavis said, 'I need to talk to Amitbhai, but my opinion is that we should get to the Governor before they do. But before I get on with that, please send a letter from the party to the Governor's office that the NCP will be supporting the BJP in forming the government. I will also send a letter claiming stake as the single-largest party and on our intent to ally with the NCP. For further formalities, we will need to prove our majority. I already have the document of signatures of my MLAs and a separate one with the signatures of the independents who are supporting us.'

Ajit replied, 'Being the legislative leader of the party, I also have in my possession the document with all my MLA's signatures. Being the NCP party whip, if I ask them to vote a certain way, they have no choice but to do so, or they risk disqualification by the Speaker.'

Fadnavis said, 'Yes, the Speaker has to be our confidant, in that case.'

Pawar pointed out, 'I don't see a reason why that cannot happen. The Speaker's election in the House is by secret ballot. My group leaders will be instructed to vote for our chosen candidate.'

'Hmm… Give me a few minutes, I will get back to you with the next steps.' Fadnavis ended the call and immediately rang Amit Shah.

Shah listened patiently to Fadnavis's updates and said, 'If we are to stake claim, it has to happen tonight. We can't risk the timing. There is no knowing that the Maha Vikas Aghadi won't stake claim first thing in the morning, even though their talks were inconclusive. Ajit and you go to the Governor with your letters; meanwhile, I will figure out how the President's Rule can be revoked. We don't have enough time to call a Union Cabinet meeting to send its recommendation to the President to revoke President's Rule. Also, I'll send Bhupendra Yadav, our elections-in-charge to help with the coordination of the swearing-in ceremony. It has to happen at the break of dawn tomorrow.'

At about half-past nine in the evening, Ajit Pawar and

Devendra Fadnavis sought an appointment with Governor Koshyari and went to the Raj Bhavan together. They submitted the letters of their respective MLA's signatures. Ajit Pawar's letter of support had 54 signatures and Fadnavis's had 105, taking the total to 159 legislators. This clearly was a majority, enough for the Governor to be convinced and take the next steps required to revoke the President's Rule.

All of the BJP's senior hierarchy got to work to make arrangements for the swearing-in ceremony to take place the next morning. They had to take great care to prevent an information leak. They kept the informed core team very small. In Delhi, after several legal consultations, Amit Shah and the prime minister took a final call to revoke the President's Rule by invoking Rule 12 of the Transaction of Business Rules, 1961. Rule 12 of the Transaction of Business Rules, 1961, empowers the Centre to revoke the proclamation of President's Rule without prior approval from the Union Cabinet. This particular clause, pertaining to 'Departure from Rules', says that 'the prime minister may in any case or classes of cases permit or condone a departure from these rules, to the extent he deems necessary'. In effect, it allows the Centre to bypass the official method of revocation of President's Rule as mentioned in the Constitution.

The notification of the revocation of President's Rule was prepared immediately. It read, 'In the exercise of the powers conferred by Clause 2 of Article 356 of the Constitution,

I, Ram Nath Kovind, President of India, hereby revoke the Proclamation issued by me under the said Article on the 12th day of November, 2019, in relation to the state of Maharashtra with effect from the 23rd day of November, 2019.' This notification was digitally signed by the officer concerned before being uploaded on the official gazette portal. As per the norms, the notification had to have been physically signed by the President before being digitally signed and uploaded, and the way it had played out indicated that the authorities concerned as well as the President had burned the midnight oil to ensure that the notification was prepared and signed on time.

23 November 2019

6.30 a.m., Raj Bhavan, Mumbai

At half-past six in the morning, preparations were on in full swing at the Governor's residence for the oath-taking ceremony. Devendra Fadnavis was to take oath as the chief minister and Ajit Pawar as the deputy chief minister. The latter called 11 of his trusted group leaders in the early hours of the morning and asked them to be present at 7.30 a.m. at B4 Bungalow, Madam Cama Road, Nariman Point, Mumbai – Dhananjay Munde's official bungalow, allotted to him because he was the leader of Opposition.

6.30 a.m., Silver Oak

Sharad Pawar and Supriya Sule got calls from the MLAs who had got wind of such an event taking place. Supriya came running down the stairs of their residence to find Sharad Pawar already on the phone. He rang up the Raj Bhavan, 'Is there an event taking place soon? I have trusted information that there is.' The Raj Bhavan informed him that no event was scheduled to take place that day.

7.50 a.m., Raj Bhavan

At exactly 7.50 a.m. in the morning, Governor Koshyari administered the oath to Fadnavis and Ajit Pawar. Even as the people of Maharashtra were waking up to face a new day, images of the oath-taking ceremony flooded the media. Immediately after the oath was administered in the presence of the BJP's core committee leaders, the wives of Fadnavis and Pawar, and some senior bureaucrats, Prime Minister Narendra Modi tweeted at 8.16 a.m.: 'Congratulations to @ Dev_Fadnavis Ji and @AjitPawarSpeaks Ji on taking oath as the CM and Deputy CM of Maharashtra respectively. I am confident they will work diligently for the bright future of Maharashtra.' Exactly 20 minutes after the prime minister's tweet, at 8.37 a.m., Amit Shah tweeted his congratulatory message in Hindi. Simultaneously, security was beefed up at the BJP headquarters, the NCP's headquarters and at the chief minister's residence, Varsha.

The news sent shockwaves through the Shiv Sena and the Congress. Supriya Sule updated her status on WhatsApp with an emotional message: 'Party and Family splits'. She followed it up minutes later with another one: 'Who do you trust in life... never felt so cheated in my life, defended him, loved him... look what I get in return.'[1]

Sharad Pawar was acutely aware of how he was likely to be perceived in the Sena and Congress ranks. They could not be blamed if they were convinced that he had a hand to play in this shocking development. Journalists thronged outside Sharad Pawar's residence wanting to know how he had orchestrated this grand game. Sharad Pawar knew it was especially important that he reassure the restive Shiv Sena cadre, who would quickly resort to violence if they believed their leader was cheated. The Congress high command too were unsure which way Sharad Pawar was swaying – they did not as yet know whether there was really a split in the NCP or if Sharad Pawar had given his blessings to his nephew to take the steps he had. But before both parties could reach out to Sharad Pawar for a clarification, Pawar called up Uddhav and said, 'Uddhav, I assure you I had no knowledge that Ajit will take this step. No matter what, I will make you the chief minister of Maharashtra.'

On further pressure from both the parties, Sharad Pawar went public with his statement and tweeted at about 9.27 a.m., 'Ajit Pawar's decision to support the BJP to form the Maharashtra government is his personal decision and not that of the Nationalist Congress Party (NCP). We place on record that we do not support or endorse this decision of his.'

Meanwhile, speaking to the media immediately after the swearing-in ceremony, Ajit Pawar had this to say: 'Maharashtra's people have not given a clear mandate to any one party. From our experiences of the last 20 years, we have seen that a two-party government is more stable than a tri-party government. The NCP–Congress had together been in power for 15 years and after that the BJP–Shiv Sena were in power for about five years. Sharad Pawar Saheb was aware of my discussions with the BJP, especially in the early days. Even as time progressed, I maintained my stand that I do not think that a tri-party government will be stable for Maharashtra.'

Fadnavis was a happy man. After all, he had finally succeeded in forming a government. Immediately after the swearing-in ceremony, he told the media, 'The people of Maharashtra had given us a clear mandate. However, our allies, the Shiv Sena, reached out to other parties and tried to ally with them, as a result of which President's Rule was imposed in the state. Maharashtra needed a stable government not a *khichdi* government.'

Predictably, social media went berserk with various memes and jokes about how Sharad Pawar and Amit Shah had together outsmarted the Congress and the Sena. Some were downright offensive and some witty and humorous, though all indicated that eventually the modern-day Chanakya, Amit Shah, had outsmarted all his opponents. The hashtag '#motabhaipolitics' began to trend. The people of the state did not seem to mind this arrangement either; there were no protests against the way events had turned out and no vocal objections either. After all, if the Sena had refused to join hands with the BJP, what choice did the BJP have but to try and rope in others in order to fulfil the people's mandate? Moreover, the elections had been fought under brand Modi, not under brand Balasaheb Thackeray.

Immediately after Sharad Pawar posted his tweet, Sanjay Raut addressed the media in Mumbai, saying, '*Ajit Pawar kal ratri paryant aamchya sobat hote. Pan te sampoorn baithaki madhye aamchya najrela najre milvun bolat navhte. Jo vyakti paap karne jaata hai, aur jis prakaar se uski najare jukti hai, us tarah se Ajit ki najare jhuki hui thi.* (Until last night, Ajit Pawar was with us. But throughout the meeting he did not look anyone in the eye. Any person who wants to sin will lower his eyes, and Ajit's eyes were lowered.) His body language was suspicious. I noticed it. Sharad Pawar Saheb noticed it too. Ajit then suddenly left the meeting midway after which his phone was switched off. We were told by a few people close to him that he was sitting in a meeting with his lawyers. Now we know who he was truly sitting with. I can confidently say that Sharad Pawar Saheb has no role to play in any of this.'

He continued in his trademark style of speaking, complete with eye-rolls and hand gestures, 'Yes, I understand that our discussions were inconclusive and got extended by a day, but that doesn't justify his actions. However, the way the Bharatiya Janata Party has misused the Raj Bhavan once again does not bode well for our democratic processes. *Satta, paisa aur masti – yeh sab ka phir ek baar gair kanooni dhang se Bharatiya Janata Party ne vaapar kiya hai.* (Power, money and mischief – once again the BJP has used these unlawfully.) Until now I held the Governor in very high regard because of his high RSS and cultural background. I always thought of him as a law-abiding individual.

'*Lekin, andhere mein paap hota hai, andhere mein dacaiti aur chori hoti hai. Maharashtra ki sarkar ko jis tarah se andhere mein shapath dilaayi gayi, yeh Chhatrapati Shivaji Maharaj ke Maharashtra ko shobha nahi deta.* (But misdeeds occur mainly at night, thefts and looting occur then too. The way the government of Maharashtra was aided to take oath in the darkness does not suit Chhatrapati Shivaji Maharaj's Maharashtra.) I would like to tell Ajit Pawar and all those MLAs who have gone with him, not Devendra Fadnavis – because the BJP can do anything for power – that Ajit Pawar and his MLAs have besmirched the reputation of Chhatrapati Shivaji Maharaj's Maharashtra. The people of Maharashtra will leave them out on the street.'[2]

After this first reaction from the Sena, Sharad Pawar, Uddhav and Ahmed Patel held extensive phone conversations where Sharad Pawar suggested that they hold a press conference together to show that they were still very much together. However, Ahmed Patel was opposed to the idea because the Congress still needed to deliberate internally if Sharad Pawar's word could be taken at face value going forward.

Before the press conference that had been scheduled for 12.30 p.m., the challenge for Sharad Pawar was to keep his people together and also get back into the fold the ones who had gone with Ajit. He phoned each of the MLAs who had attended the ceremony at Raj Bhavan and threatened them with disqualification if they disobeyed the party's wishes. He asked them to meet him immediately, regardless of where they were located at the time. Not wanting to further anger Sharad Pawar, three of the MLAs returned immediately. The rest weighed their options, some possibly even considering a switch over to the BJP. A few minutes before the conference, Nawab Malik went on record to clarify to those asking how Ajit Pawar had the signatures of support of NCP MLAs in his possession. He said, 'The signatures that Ajit Pawar possessed were those that we had taken from the MLAs for attendance. They have been misused as the basis to prove majority and take oath.'

When the time for the press conference arrived, Ahmed Patel and the Congress still had not come around to the idea of joining it. Uddhav and Sharad Pawar, however, decided not to lose precious time and went ahead with it.

12.30 p.m., Yashwantrao Chavan Centre

About 20 leaders of the NCP and the Shiv Sena settled themselves on the stage, looking grim, upset and angry, as Sharad Pawar began to address the press.

'The Congress, the NCP and the Shiv Sena had been in talks and in fact almost concluded them regarding government formation in Maharashtra,' he said. 'The three parties had decided to come together and form a government. However, this morning at 6.30, I was woken up by a phone call and told that there was a meeting at the Raj Bhavan. About 10 or 11 of our MLAs had also been present at the Raj Bhavan during the oath-taking ceremony. Let me clearly tell you that the NCP does not support Ajit's decision to ally with the BJP.

'None of those 10 or 11 MLAs who went to the Raj Bhavan went there to attend the oath-taking ceremony. They were misled. A true NCP MLA will never join hands with the BJP in the state. Those MLAs who went to Raj Bhavan with Ajit Pawar unknowingly will not face any disciplinary action. However, those who chose this knowingly will certainly face action. In our country, we have an anti-defection law due to which MLAs who switch parties in this manner could face disqualification. Even in the bypolls, they will not get the support of the people, and the Congress, NCP and Shiv Sena will together ensure that they are defeated. Present here are three of those 11 MLAs who came to me as soon as they exited the Raj Bhavan.'

The mic was passed on to one of the MLAs seated right behind Sharad Pawar. He identified himself as Dr Rajendra Shinde. He said, 'Late last night around midnight, Ajit Dada called me and asked me to come to B4 bungalow at seven the next morning. B4 bungalow is the official residence of Dhananjay Munde, the leader of the Opposition. As Ajit Dada was the legislative leader of the party, I followed his instructions and reached the venue on time.

'In about 10 to 15 minutes, another 10 or 11 MLAs gathered. We were all told that we had to head to Raj Bhavan for a meeting. When we reached Raj Bhavan, Chandrakant Dada Patil and Girish Mahajan of the BJP were already present along with Shri Devendra Fadnavis. Immediately, the honourable Governor arrived and the oath-taking ceremony started, where Devendra Fadnavis was administered oath as the CM and Ajit Dada as the deputy CM. As soon as the ceremony ended, we were asked to disperse. None of us knew why we were asked to go to Raj Bhavan. Immediately, I came to Pawar Saheb to make my intent of supporting the NCP and Pawar Saheb clear.' The other two NCP MLAs present confirmed this version.

The mic was then passed on to a grim-looking Uddhav.

He started by saying, 'Honourable Pawar Saheb has in very clear words placed the reality of the situation in front of you all. Whatever game is going on in our country in the name of democracy is shameful. This new Hindutva is not working. In the past, there were accusations on them of EVMs [electronic voting machines] being fiddled with. And now, with such acts, these people are showing that they're stuck to the *kursi* with Fevicol.'

'We have been blamed that we have disrespected the people's mandate. As you all already know, whatever the Shiv Sena does, it does openly. Our politics is not one that is played in the middle of the night. Whatever we do, we do in the middle of the day. *Tumhi jo karto he manse fodoon karto and aamhi jo karto te jodun karto.* (What you do is by breaking ranks, and what we do is by uniting ranks.) But we are blamed for disrespecting the people's mandate. You have tried to form a government in this manner in Bihar, Haryana, Karnataka.'

'We are all followers of Chhatrapati Shivaji Maharaj. History tells us what Maharaj did when someone tried to stab him in the back. All these games of using the Governor's powers and calling the Union Cabinet urgently to invoke President's Rule or even using special powers to revoke it, they remind us of the surgical strikes that were conducted in Pakistan. Except in this case the surgical strikes are done in Shivaji's Maharashtra. All I can say is that we will act according to the law and the three parties of ours are in this together.'

Sharad Pawar took charge of the mic again and opened the floor to questions. On being probed whether he would disqualify and suspend Ajit Pawar, he said, 'This decision is not mine alone. The party's leadership committee will debate over it and collectively come to a decision regarding the disciplinary action to be taken at the legislator's meeting today.'

A couple of hours after the oath-taking ceremony, Sanjay Raut once again faced the media cameras. He said, 'The BJP has blackmailed Ajit Pawar by using these central agencies. We have all this information with us and will expose it soon.'

Meanwhile, Sharad Pawar sat around with his team of legislators and took swift action to bring back the NCP men who had strayed. There were reports that apart from the five who had returned to the party's fold, there were others who were about to board a flight to New Delhi to be kept under the BJP's protection. Upon receiving this information from an MNS party worker who headed a union of aviation employees at the Mumbai airport, Uddhav activated the Sena cadre in Mumbai. He immediately dispatched Milind Narvekar and Eknath Shinde to bring back the MLAs from the airport.

A couple of hours later, the duo returned with two MLAs who had been about to board their flight.[3] Another piece of information arrived that three more MLAs had managed to fly out to Gurgaon, where the BJP had arranged for their accommodation in a five-star hotel. According to those who witnessed the call, Sharad Pawar called up Haryana's former Congress chief minister Bhupinder Singh Hooda and ensured that the NCP MLAs were evicted from the hotel and immediately sent back to Maharashtra. He even activated his party cadre of student karyakartas in the state to facilitate the evacuation on ground.[4]

The issue of Dhananjay Munde going rogue was a problem. Being a senior leader, he had many friends in the party. Sharad Pawar was livid when he found out that that morning Dhananjay Munde had offered his residence for the NCP MLAs to gather before they were led to Raj Bhavan. Although he had not gone to Raj Bhavan, he had gone incommunicado after the ceremony.

People present with Sharad Pawar during this time said that they had very rarely seen Sharad Pawar this angry. The leader sent a clear message to Dhananjay Munde through his friends that the latter should prepare to face severe consequences if he didn't return to the patriarch's fold. Finally, Dhananjay Munde yielded. Sanjay Raut came back to the media and said that they had been able to establish contact with Dhananjay Munde and that he was expected to show up at any moment to join the ongoing legislators' meet. Indeed, minutes later, Munde arrived at the meeting, where Sharad Pawar and Chhagan Bhujbal unleashed their wrath on him.[5] Munde explained to his irate colleagues that he was not party to Ajit Pawar's plan and had, in fact, been sleeping all morning until 1 p.m., which was why he had not answered any calls. According to sources, he had a video shot by his team showing them breaking into his room to wake him up after they had received several calls from the party seniors enquiring about his whereabouts. In a later interview, clarifying that he had not offered his bungalow to Ajit Pawar to gather the MLAs and plan a breakaway faction, he said,

'My bungalow is an open house. At times, it is like a bus stand and is widely used for party work.'[6]

By the end of that day, 13 NCP MLAs who were with Ajit Pawar also returned to the NCP.

Meanwhile, the Congress too held a press conference. It was helmed by Ahmed Patel and K.C. Venugopal, along with a few top Congress state leaders. Ahmed Patel said, 'Friends, as you all know, early in the morning today, without any band, *baaja* and *baaraat*, an oath was administered to the chief minister and the deputy chief minister. It is a black day in the history of Maharashtra... Barring the ANI, no one from the media was called.

'*Mujhe boo aa rahi hai* (I can smell) that something is amiss. Nothing can be more shameful than this. People of India, people of Maharashtra are those who have faith in democracy and the Constitution. Whatever has happened and the way it has happened disregarding the democratic processes and the provisions of the Constitution, *main samajhta hoon ki democracy aur Constitution ki dhajjiya udaayi gayi hai* (I believe that democracy and the Constitution have been mocked). We condemn this act.

'The day after Uddhavji called the Congress president, Soniaji, with the proposal to ally with us and the NCP, we immediately got into action. We started the process the very next day, taking into confidence all our colleagues. When Sharad Pawarji came to New Delhi last week, we had two meetings at his residence and we were on board with everything. There were a few points which were important to discuss with the Shiv Sena, which is why we came to Mumbai and held a meeting yesterday. It was a calm meeting with a couple of points that needed more discussions. To hold those discussions, we were to meet again today at 12.30 p.m. But before that could happen, *aaj subah ka jo kaand hua uski aalochna karne ke liye mere paas koi shabd nahi hai* (the act that took place in the morning, I have no words to describe it).'

He went on to say that the Congress would fight the situation both politically and legally.

The day progressed and at the NCP legislators' meeting, the party unanimously sacked Ajit Pawar as the leader of party's legislature and replaced him with Jayant Patil. However, they did not suspend him from the party itself. The resolution passed at the meeting also revoked Ajit Pawar's right to issue a whip. A party whip has the right to command the MLAs on the floor of the house about which way voting should go. The party whip can discipline outliers if any, by asking the Speaker of the House to disqualify them. The discretion whether or not to disqualify the outlier MLAs lies solely with the Speaker, but the Speaker does consider the appeal of the party whip. Usually, this is the kind of power that is the most abused in political situations in India.

Usually, the Speaker is selected by means of a secret ballot after being nominated by the majority party and those MLAs from other parties in the House who officially or unofficially support the majority party. In the event that a faction of the MLAs of an opposition party choose to break out and support another party on the floor of the House, the party whip appeals to the Speaker to disqualify the MLAs. However, if the Speaker enjoys the confidence of the majority party and inadvertently the outlier MLAs from other parties, the Speaker does not immediately disqualify those MLAs. This enables the party in majority to add more numbers and, more often than not, their majority status is proven on the floor of the House.

In this case, the NCP sacked Ajit Pawar as its legislative party leader as well as revoked his rights to issue a whip. This would mean that he would not be able to direct the NCP MLAs to vote in favour of the BJP. The legislative party leader was now Jayant Patil and he would choose to issue a whip for his party MLAs to vote in favour of the Congress–NCP–Shiv Sena combine, thus destabilizing the newly formed Fadnavis–Ajit Pawar government.

Meanwhile, congratulatory messages kept pouring in for Devendra Fadnavis and Ajit Pawar from political bigwigs and official celebrations had commenced at the BJP party office in Mumbai. Some of the BJP leaders took the opportunity to attack the Sena all guns blazing. Chandrakant Patil told the press who had arrived to cover the celebrations, 'The people voted for the BJP–Shiv Sena alliance. Together we got 161 seats. But from the first day, the Sena has been discussing alternatives. At least now Sanjay Raut should shut up. He has ruined his party.'

Girish Mahajan, minister of irrigation and water resources

in the Fadnavis Cabinet, also tweeted that with Ajit Pawar's the support the BJP would comfortably cross the mark of 170 MLAs on the floor of the House when they had to prove their majority on the floor before 30 November.

By the evening, the Shiv Sena, the Congress and the NCP together moved the Supreme Court urgently for a joint petition against the 'illegal usurpation of power' by the BJP in Maharashtra leading to a 'hurried and makeshift' swearing-in ceremony that installed Devendra Fadnavis as chief minister. The court's registry accepted the plea at 8.23 p.m. A bench was constituted, comprising of Justices N.V. Ramana, Ashok Bhushan and Sanjiv Khanna, and a hearing was scheduled for the following day (a Sunday) at 11.30 a.m. The petition made the Union ministry of home affairs, the State of Maharashtra and the deputy chief minister, Ajit Pawar, respondents in the case.

The petition contended, 'There is nothing in the public domain in what manner Shri Devendra Fadnavis and/or the BJP had staked claim to power between the intervening night of 22.11.2019 and 23.11.2019. Further, there is no material in the public domain to show that Shri Devendra Fadnavis had carried letters of support of 144 MLAs. All the MLAs of the Shiv Sena, NCP and Congress are completely and solidly with the alliance except for Shri Ajit Pawar. The Governor's action shows his partisanship and he has made a mockery of his high constitutional office.

'What was the hurry and hot haste to revoke the President's Rule at 5.47 a.m. and administer oath at around 8 a.m., barely two and a half hours later. It is doubtful that the Governor applied his mind to the claim, if any, made by Mr Fadnavis. He should have proceeded carefully especially in light of the fact that the Congress–NCP–Shiv Sena combine commanding 154 MLAs had made their intention to form the government only the previous night.'

The petition further stated, 'The Governor's actions between the intervening night of 22.11.2019 and 23.11.2019 culminating in the swearing-in on the morning of 23.11.2019 are a textbook example of the Governor acting at the behest of a political party in power at the Centre. Facing the prospect of a non-BJP government staking claim to power, the BJP in the intervening night of 22.11.2019 and 23.11.2019 resorted to political machinations in an attempt to install a completely unconstitutional BJP government in the State.'

13

SHOW OF STRENGTH

24 November 2019

Just before the Supreme Court was to hear the petition filed by the Congress–NCP–Sena combine, advocate Ashish Shelar, head of the BJP's Mumbai unit and an MLA from the constituency of Bandra, told the media, 'The removal of Ajit Pawar as the legislative party leader is invalid. The letter of support to the Governor was given by Ajit Pawar as leader of the NCP's legislature. Besides, the Sena–NCP–Congress plea in the Supreme Court does not challenge the 30 October appointment of Ajit Pawar as the legislative party leader.'

The BJP consulted its legal team which opined that since Ajit Pawar was the leader of the NCP's party legislative when the letter of majority was submitted to the Governor, only he had the right to issue the whip to his party regardless of the fact that the party had replaced him with Jayant Patil.

Morning, the Supreme Court of India, New Delhi

The BJP appointed advocate Mukul Rohatgi to represent Devendra Fadnavis, and advocate Tushar Mehta to represent the Centre. Lawyers Abhishek Manu Singhvi and Kapil Sibal were appointed to represent the tripartite alliance.

When the arguments began, Kapil Sibal said, 'Apologies for the hearing being held on Sunday, but we are not the ones to blame. In the formation of the [state] government, governors have some discretion as has been decided by the judgements of this court. It appears that the Governor is acting directly under the orders of a political party. The act of the Governor smacks of bias, is mala fide, contrary to all norms.'

Mukul Rohatgi countered the above by stating that the case should have first gone through jurisdiction 226, which gives the high court jurisdiction over such matters.

As the proceedings progressed, Abhishek Manu Singhvi said, 'The Governor should have waited for the swearing in on the floor of the House after the floor test, before going ahead with the swearing-in ceremony.' He read out a recently delivered judgement on a similar case in Karnataka and urged the bench for a floor test to be held the next day. 'If the floor test is ordered for tomorrow, larger issues may come back to the Supreme Court later. How is it possible for someone claiming majority yesterday to shy away from a floor test today? If an immediate floor test is ordered, it will not be an "invasive adversarial order" at all,' Singhvi contended.

Advocate Rohatgi countered this with, 'Two or three days' time must be given for us to file responses. No tearing hurry. If the petitioners had support, they should have formed the government in the 17 days before President's Rule was imposed. A Governor's action is immune to judicial review and intervention according to Article 361 of the Constitution of India. There are some aspects of individual discretion of the President or Governor. Here, the Governor's decision cannot be under judicial review. The petition is directed against the Governor. There is complete bar on any action against the Governor. What the Governor did is immune to judicial review.'

From the bench, Justice Ramana reminded the room about the issue at hand. 'These issues are already settled. The issue in this case is to prove majority on the floor of the House.'

Advocate Rohatgi replied, 'The petitioners' prayer says the Supreme Court has to direct the Governor to invite them to form the government.'

Justice Ramana answered humorously, 'Mr Rohatgi, in this court, the sky is the limit for asking for prayers.'

Advocate Rohatgi pleaded again, 'That's why we want three days. The petitioners moved suddenly at night, didn't even wait for the next day, and disturbed the court. Everyone knows that the Supreme Court cannot direct the Governor to invite the petitioner. The House respects the court and the court must respect the House. Suppose the House passes orders that the Supreme Court must dispose all cases within two years!'

Justice Ramana shot back, 'We respect the House.'

Advocate Rohatgi concluded, 'This petition is not maintainable. The petitioners were sleeping for three weeks. If the Supreme Court issues a notice, we will file a reply. Two or three days' time must be given to us to bring on record the facts. Even the Speaker cannot be directed by the Supreme Court. We must be given time and be allowed to spend our Sunday in peace.'

The bench then adjudicated and passed an order. 'Issue involved is that the Governor's decision dated 23/11/19 inviting the BJP to form government is unconstitutional. For the adjudication of this issue – we request Tushar Mehta to produce the two letters by tomorrow morning. First, the letter by the Governor inviting the BJP to form government and, second, the letter of support placed by Fadnavis. Appropriate orders will be passed by the court at 10.30 a.m. tomorrow.'

11.00 a.m., Raj Bhavan, Mumbai

Senior NCP leader Jayant Patil arrived at Raj Bhavan with a letter for the Governor informing him that Ajit Pawar had been sacked as the leader of the party legislative and that he had been appointed as the new leader.

After Sharad Pawar's quick and aggressive action, most NCP MLAs from the Ajit Pawar camp had returned to the Renaissance Mumbai Convention Centre Hotel, where the rest of the NCP MLAs were holed up.

Ajit Pawar's Brother's Residence, Churchgate, Mumbai

Ajit Pawar spent most of the day at his brother's residence meeting top-rung NCP leaders who continued to plead with him to return to the party.[1]

At 5 p.m. that evening, Ajit Pawar tweeted, 'I am in the NCP and will always be in the NCP and Sharad Pawar Saheb is our leader. Our BJP–NCP alliance shall provide a stable government in Maharashtra for the next five years which will work sincerely for the welfare of the state and its people.' He concluded with the words, 'There is absolutely no need to worry. All is well. However, a little patience is required. Thank you very much for all your support.'

Once again, his tweets threw the NCP, the Sena and the Congress cadres into confusion. From his words it sounded like there were MLAs in the NCP, housed at the Renaissance Mumbai Convention Centre Hotel, who were willing to vote in favour of the Fadnavis–Ajit Pawar government on the floor of the House.

In order to dispel the confusion, Sharad Pawar sprang into action once again. Less than an hour after his nephew's tweet the senior Pawar posted, 'There is no question of forming an alliance with the Maharashtra BJP. The NCP has unanimously decided to ally with the Shiv Sena and the Congress to form the government. Shri Ajit Pawar's statement is false and misleading in order to create confusion and false perceptions among the people.'

Immediately after that, Sharad Pawar left his residence to arrive at the Renaissance Mumbai Convention Centre Hotel. He was joined there by Uddhav. They addressed a full house of NCP MLAs and assured them that there was no doubt that the three-party combine would win the trust vote on the floor of the House and form the government.

Later in the evening, amidst security concerns that the BJP

was sending its men to the hotel to poach MLAs, the NCP shifted the men to the Grand Hyatt. The Shiv Sena put up its MLAs in The Lalit Hotel and the Congress put up its cadre at the JW Marriott. The three hotels were 200 metres apart from each other, near the international airport and controlled by the Shiv Sena's union of hotel workers.

Such a strict watch was kept on the MLAs that one of them complained he was being followed to the gym when he went for a workout, while another was irritated at a Shiv Sena party worker who demanded to check his phone, infringing on his privacy.

When Sharad Pawar arrived at the hotel, he specifically met the MLAs who had been a part of Ajit Pawar's breakaway team and demanded answers from them. According to an eyewitness account of the scene, Sharad Pawar was fuming and did not hesitate to make his feelings known.[2]

Later at Night, Varsha

That night, Ajit Pawar and Fadnavis had a closed-door, one-on-one meeting to discuss what the way forward could be.

While discussing the ongoing apex court proceedings, Fadnavis said, 'Dada, as you know, Mukul Rohatgi has been assigned to me by Amitbhai. I have great faith in him. He has informed me that he has included in his response, several precedents from past judgements of the Supreme Court. In those judgements, the court had adjudicated that the trust vote on the floor of the House must be carried out according to the "rules of business". "Rules of business" would mean that the Speaker will be appointed by a secret ballot. Several of the NCP leaders who are on your side can vote fearlessly for our candidate. If the Speaker is our man, your MLAs do not have to worry about being disqualified. After the election of the Speaker, "rules of business" would also mean that the majority in the House must be established by a voice vote. Even if Jayant Patil, the new legislative party leader, appeals to disqualify the MLAs who vote in our favour, the Speaker will reject his appeal or at least defer it. Rohatgiji says that the sense he has got from the bench is that they will adjudicate based on precedents.'

Ajit Pawar looked relieved. 'Yes, this will certainly work in our favour. My men are still on our side regardless of Pawar Saheb's efforts. Several of the top leaders who are Pawar Saheb's closest confidants will also vote in our favour. There can even be a situation where we may get some last-minute converts.'

The two then moved on to reviewing state business and signing immediate orders to release a ₹5,300-crore contingency fund providing relief to farmers in the state hit by unseasonal rains.

25 November 2019, Mumbai

Jitendra Awhad, a senior NCP leader, rang up Milind Narvekar and casually floated the idea that the MLAs of all the three parties be made to assemble at one venue to display a 'show of strength', mostly to boost the morale of the cadre and to create some noise.[3] Milind liked the idea and immediately sounded out Uddhav, while Awhad discussed it with Sharad

Pawar. Once both leaders were on board with the idea, they floated it with the Congress leadership, who agreed as well.

Within a few hours, preparations were made to bring the Sena and Congress MLAs to the Grand Hyatt, where the NCP MLAs were staying. A dinner event was organized in the ballroom of the hotel.

At the event, the MLAs of the three parties held up banners that said, 'WE ARE 162.' They took photos with each other and put them up on social media. As if directly addressing the BJP, Uddhav said, 'We will be in power not just for five years, but together for 30 more years after that. We will bury those who are hungry for power. The BJP is desperately clinging on to power, but we will come back stronger. The party won't tolerate any underhand tricks. The BJP has been with us for 30 years and should know what we are capable of. In the past 30 years, the BJP has only seen our friendship. If they create more problems, we will show them our might.'

Addressing rumours doing the rounds that Ajit Pawar would get them to vote in favour of the BJP and that if it did not happen the MLAs would be disqualified, Sharad Pawar took to the stage to clear the air that Ajit Pawar had no right to issue a whip to the MLAs to vote in favour of the BJP. He said, 'Tomorrow, the Supreme Court will decide on the date for the vote of confidence. The Governor will have no option but to call the BJP. Unlike Manipur or Goa, this is Maharashtra. We won't allow anything wrong to happen. We say what is right and what is wrong. We have the capacity to teach the BJP a lesson. We will not allow the constitutional process to be destroyed. We will make history.

'The three parties will not accept any underhand dealings and we will be ready for any strong-arm tactics. We have the Shiv Sena with us. I don't think I need to say anything more. The Centre has been using all kinds of tricks to hang on to power in different states in the country and now a minority government is in power in Maharashtra. The country is seeing for the first time to what extent the BJP is using government machinery to come to power in different states like Karnataka, Goa and Manipur. I assure you that you will not be disqualified and I take personal responsibility for it. I have got written opinions from former senior officers who have worked in the Parliament and in the Maharashtra legislature that once a leader is removed from the position [of leader of the party's legislature), he cannot issue a whip.'

This was Sharad Pawar at his vintage best. Not even 10 days had passed since he had made up his mind to support the BJP, and he had just about a fortnight ago helped the BJP invoke President's Rule in the state by not giving the letter of support to the Sena in time. In just about a fortnight, he had turned in a different direction forming new alliances with the Sena and refreshing those he had had with old friends like the Congress. The 162 MLAs then took an oath, standing up with one hand outstretched in the front and the other on their hearts, saying that they would not 'fall prey to any inducements and would obey the party's stand and would remain faithful to it'. The moment made for great photographs in the media.

14

THE COURT INTERVENES

26 November 2019

The Supreme Court of India, New Delhi

On the matter before them involving the political situation in Maharashtra, the Supreme Court adjudicated and passed an order that referred to several past orders.

> We may note that in the present case, oath has not been administered to the elected members even though a month has elapsed since the declaration of election results. In such emergent facts and circumstances, to curtail unlawful practices such as horse-trading, to avoid uncertainty and to effectuate smooth running of democracy by ensuring a stable Government, we are of the considered opinion that it is necessary to pass certain interim directions in this case. In this context, it is necessary and expedient to conduct the floor test as soon as possible to determine whether the Chief Minister, who was administered the oath of office, has the support of the majority or not. Since the elected

members of the Legislative Assembly are yet to take oath as specified in the Third Schedule of the Constitution, and the Speaker is also yet to be elected, we request the Governor of the State of Maharashtra to ensure that a floor test be held on 27.11.2019.

The following procedure is to be followed for conducting the floor test:

- Pro tem Speaker shall be solely appointed for the aforesaid agenda immediately.
- All the elected members shall take oath on 27.11.2019, which exercise should be completed before 5 p.m.
- Immediately thereafter, the pro tem Speaker shall conduct the floor test in order to ascertain whether the Respondent No. 3 has the majority, and these proceedings shall be conducted in accordance with law. The floor test will not be conducted by secret ballot.
- The proceedings have to be live telecast, and appropriate arrangements are to be made to ensure the same.

As soon as the court's judgement came in, Fadnavis spoke to Ajit Pawar. 'Dada, this is not what was expected of the judgment. This poses several challenges for us. The first challenge will be that the pro tem Speaker will not be our man. He will have to be appointed by the Governor after consultations with everybody. Additionally, the floor test will not be conducted by a voice vote, but by a show of hands. The MLAs in the NCP who are on our side will not and should not have to risk their MLA positions. Unfortunately, this is not an ideal scenario for us and we simply cannot go ahead with our plan.'

Ajit Pawar felt disillusioned and disappointed. Over the last 80 hours, the top brass of the NCP, namely Jayant Patil, Chhagan Bhujbal and Praful Patel had come to meet him and tried to convince him to respect Sharad Pawar's decision of not allying with the BJP and coming back into the party fold, but he had held his ground.

He told Fadnavis, 'Devendraji, I am still willing to do this, if you want to go ahead.'

Fadnavis replied, 'This is not the right time, Ajit Dada. You should resign. And, following your resignation, I will [do the same], citing lack of numbers to achieve a majority to pass the floor test.'

Now, Ajit Pawar was in a dilemma. Even if he wanted to return to the NCP fold, what respect would he have left among its members? How would he face Pawar Saheb? Coincidently, just minutes later, Sadanand Sule, Supriya's husband, came to meet Ajit Pawar. He convinced the conflicted man that the time wasn't right to rebel and that the party and the family were wholeheartedly willing to accept him back – and that he would be welcomed back with his reputation and political position intact. Sadanand dialled the phone and connected Ajit Pawar to Sharad Pawar's wife, Pratibha *tai*. Pratibha *tai* warmly asked her nephew to return to the family and the party.[1] She asked him not to hesitate at all if he wanted to return. This was the opportunity for Ajit to trace back his steps and now he knew what he had to do. He accompanied Sadanand Sule to Sharad Pawar's residence, where the family had a meeting.

Immediately after that the meeting, Ajit Pawar sent his resignation from the post of the deputy chief minister of

Maharashtra to the Governor. Later that afternoon, Devendra Fadnavis resigned as well, and the government – all of 80 hours in existence – came crumbling down.

After the fall of the Devendra Fadnavis–Ajit Pawar government, several theories began to be floated as to the way the events had unfolded. Almost all of them led to one crucial question: Was Sharad Pawar the mastermind behind the entire sequence of occurrences?

It was difficult for many to believe that any kind of political machination could have remained concealed from a man as sharp as Sharad Pawar. But if he knew that Ajit Pawar would break ranks, why had he chosen to keep his lips sealed? Was it so that he could establish a clear line of succession in his party? For many years, ever since Supriya Sule was called back by her father from Singapore in 2006, where she resided with her family, there had existed a battle for succession. Sharad Pawar was seen to be grooming his daughter for a larger role in the party. Ajit Pawar, on the other hand, had been the one taking crucial party decisions for many years, raising funds for elections and distributing electoral tickets. His son, Parth, too had first been denied a ticket and then given one only after Ajit Pawar had protested. Even then, Parth had not received the kind of support from Sharad Pawar for the Lok Sabha elections as his nephew would have expected. By letting Ajit Pawar make a mistake and falter, observers wondered, had Sharad Pawar wanted to assert that Ajit was not the chosen one to continue the Pawar legacy?

Ever since the Maha Vikas Aghadi government began to function, there has been no doubt whatsoever that it is held together by the 80-year-old Sharad Pawar. The fact that *Saamna* chose to carry his interview, breaking away from its tradition of only carrying interviews of members of the Thackeray clan, says it all. Many political observers believe that the Maha Vikas Aghadi will crumble like a cookie if Sharad Pawar allows his tight grip on it to loosen. The question remains for how long he can sustain his grip.

28 November 2019
Shivaji Park, Mumbai

The Shiv Sainiks made arrangements for a grand ceremony to induct Chief Minister Uddhav Thackeray at the very venue where Balasaheb Thackeray's last rites were performed. Huge crowds of Sainiks gathered for the event and prominent leaders of political parties from across the country were sent invitations. Industrialists, politicians and celebrities alike made themselves available for the event. Both Sonia and Rahul Gandhi were conspicuous by their absence, while, with Fadnavis and Chandrakant Patil attending the ceremony, the BJP was conspicuous by its presence. As the crowd roared in support of Uddhav, he took oath as the chief minister of Maharashtra.

At this point the Maha Vikas Aghadi could only agree on six names, two from each party to take oath as ministers in the government.

15

A GOVERNMENT IN (IN)ACTION

1 December till date
Teething Issues

For over a month after its inception, the Cabinet of the Maha Vikas Aghadi government in Maharashtra could not be expanded as the allies were not in agreement with each other. Across the three parties, important leaders felt left out or insulted that they were not given prime Cabinet berths. Eventually, when the Cabinet expansion took place on 30 December, it reeked of dynastic politics as out of the 43 new ministers who were inducted, 19 belonged to families who have enjoyed political clout for many years.

The first few months were particularly rough for Uddhav. A novice at occupying a formal government position, he is known to have walked into meetings and asked to be briefed by bureaucrats before taking decisions. For the first couple of months, during the hours that he was in office, he would invite a single department and its bureaucrats for long meetings in order to understand ongoing projects and schemes, which affected daily government functions of different departments.

In the Cabinet expansion that took place, Ajit Pawar was given the prime post of deputy chief minister and minister of finance. He had been welcomed back into the Maharashtra Vidhan Bhavan with a hug from his cousin Supriya Sule just a few days after his short-lived association with the BJP. It seemed all was finally well in Pawar-land.

Never the bride, always the bridesmaid, Ajit Pawar is said to be the one who has a hold on the state's administration, albeit from behind the curtains for the moment. It could be that he is carefully biding his time until he can resurface with a bang. Starting his day at half-past six in the morning and working until the wee hours of the night, Ajit Pawar is considered in political circles to be the *karta-dharta*, the power centre, of the Maha Vikas Aghadi government. Apart from the fact that as the finance minister of the state he controls its purse strings, Ajit Pawar is skilled at his job and has decades of experience behind him of running a government as a deputy chief minister. On 2 February 2020, *Saamna* published an interview of Uddhav in which he said that the steering wheel of Maharashtra was in his hands, indicating perhaps that he was in absolute charge of affairs in the state regardless of the criticism about his leadership capabilities. A day later, on Uddhav's sixty-second birthday, Ajit Pawar tweeted a birthday wish to him with a picture of the two on a golf cart, with the latter at the steering wheel.[1]

Meanwhile, sensing the ideological gap left by Uddhav and

the Sena's new association with secular parties and perceived abandonment of the Hindutva ideology, Raj Thackeray leapt at the opportunity. In a hurried move, without wasting any time, he unveiled a new saffron flag for the Maharashtra Navanirman Sena (MNS) which bears at its centre a *rajmudra* (a royal seal used during the times of Shivaji). At the plenary meet of his party held in Goregaon on 23 January 2020, he aggressively reminded the public of his and the party's commitment to hardcore Hindutva ideals.

100 Days of Ideological Differences

It is usual practice for a new government to celebrate its first 100 days in office by announcing its most successful policies and projects. However, the Maha Vikas Aghadi, fraught with ideological differences, was not able to carry out much developmental work in its first 100 days and in the period that followed.

The biggest challenges for the Maha Vikas Aghadi has come in the form of the Citizenship Amendment Act (CAA), the National Register of Citizens (NRC) and the National Population Register (NPR). The CAA is a law that gives an individual immunity from persecution for being an illegal migrant into India and also gives him or her an opportunity to become a citizen of the country in a six-year time period. However, access to this opportunity is dependent on three conditions: first, an individual must be from Pakistan, Afghanistan or Bangladesh; second, the individual must be from one of only six religious communities – Hindu, Sikh,

Christian, Buddhist, Jain or Parsi; and third, the individual should have come to India before 31 December 2014. The NRC is meant to be an exercise to identify undocumented migrants and differentiate them from India's citizens, and that this will be based on the NPR. This requires individuals in India to prove they are citizens of the country. In the case of the NRC, people who will be able to prove their Indian citizenship will be retained in the national register and those who are undocumented will be left out. As for the CAA, it basically says that if you are a person coming from these three countries and these six religions, then you get fast-track citizenship of India and protection under its laws.

With protests raging across the country based on the perception that the CAA and NRC were discriminatory exercises against the Muslim community, ideologically opposed parties like the Hindutvavadi Shiv Sena and the secular Congress and the NCP continue to find it extremely difficult to agree on a common position. On 22 February 2020, when Uddhav asserted that he would go ahead and implement the CAA and the NPR in Maharashtra,[2] his allies panicked and asked Uddhav to reconsider his decision.[3] The Congress and the NCP put in place a special committee comprising six ministers from the three coalition partners, that they said would 'recommend' the correct stand for the government to take, thus nullifying Uddhav's stance and averting a political fallout.

Another major issue that cropped up was the resolution to the Bhima Koregaon riots. Violence broke out in Bhima Koregaon village near Pune on 1 January 2018, between

Dalits and Marathas, a day after an event in Pune called the Elgar Parishad that was organized to commemorate the Battle of Bhima Koregaon in 1818 between the East India Company and the Peshwa faction of the Maratha Confederacy. Several Left-leaning activists were arrested by the Pune police. Some of the activists had delivered strongly worded anti-establishment speeches at the Elgar Parishad event. The Pune police's charge sheet not only accused the activists of having links with Maoist rebels but also stated that one of those activists had hatched a plan to assassinate the prime minister. Meanwhile, two self-styled right-wing leaders – Sambhaji Bhide and Milind Ekbote – were accused of instigating the violence that broke out the day after the Elgar Parishad, based on eyewitness accounts.[4]

In January 2020, the Union government, expressing their distrust of the Maha Vikas Aghadi, transferred the probe from the Pune police to the National Investigation Agency (NIA). While initially the Maha Vikas Aghadi was opposed to the case being shifted to the NIA, Uddhav Thackeray, in an attempt to reaffirm his party's fast disappearing Hindutva roots, came around and gave his consent for this to be done without consulting their allies. Sharad Pawar and the NCP publicly criticized Uddhav for his action and proposed to set up a parallel probe by establishing a special investigation team to look into it. Uddhav had no choice but to let his ally have its way.[5]

In yet another matter, Nawab Malik proposed in one of his speeches during an ongoing session in the House that the Maha Vikas Aghadi government would provide 5 per cent reservation quota to Muslims in educational institutions.[6] Struggling to keep its footing within its hardcore Hindutvavadi voter base, the Shiv Sena, immediately rejected the idea saying that the chief minister had not received any such proposal till then.[7]

During the months that have followed, several such ideological differences have taken centre stage in the functioning of the Maha Vikas Aghadi government. For instance, in a speech at an election rally in Jharkhand, Rahul Gandhi condemned the BJP for ignoring the rape of a woman by a party MLA and said, 'PM Modi used to say "Make in India", but nowadays wherever you look, it is "Rape in India".' His comment drew the ire of the BJP, which aggressively demanded an apology for mocking the Prime Minister. In response to this, Rahul Gandhi stuck to his guns and refused to apologize stating, in another rally, 'My name is Rahul Gandhi, not Rahul Savarkar. I will not apologize.'[8] Veer Savarkar (Vinayak Damodar Savarkar) is an ideologue for right-wing parties and the Hindutva ideology. Rahul Gandhi had repeatedly mocked Savarkar in his speeches during the run-up to the Lok Sabha polls, saying that the freedom fighter had apologized to the British to get out of jail. If Balasaheb had been alive, a remark of this nature made about an ideologue like Savarkar would probably have had severe consequences on the alliance. But in this instance, the Sainiks, in spite of being staunch supporters of Savarkar, had to swallow their wrath and pride for the sake of the stability of the government. For an alliance formed of parties with ideological differences, the best path to ensure stability would have been to stay away from contentious ideological issues. Instead, the first 100 days were marred by exactly such problems.

As the government completed 100 days, it seemed to the political class, the bureaucrats as well as the people of the state that development was not on the Maha Vikas Aghadi's agenda. The budget that Ajit Pawar presented in the March assembly session was an incomplete one. In terms of leaders discussing their vision for the state's development, no breakthroughs were reported in the media. It remained the same old talk of infighting, stalling projects and politicking.

In fact, the overall impression has been that the alliance has ended up stalling the infrastructure projects that the Fadnavis government had undertaken. When Fadnavis had been at the helm, the government had sped up the construction of the Mumbai metro railway system and promised to complete it by the year 2024. In the original construction plan, Line 3, or the Aqua of the system, would connect Colaba in south Mumbai to SEEPZ in the north central region of the city. For this line, a metro shed was to be built in a locality called Aarey Colony once the technical teams assessed all the available and feasible options. Although the construction of the metro had faced opposition from environmentalists and activists from its inception citing the loss of green cover and the cutting down of trees in various regions, the shed to be constructed in Aarey Colony faced a larger protest. Locating the metro shed here was crucial to the smooth functioning of the ambitious Mumbai metro project and had first been approved by the Mumbai High Court, then by the Supreme Court and finally the Green Tribunal.

At the time, despite being in the government, the Shiv Sena too had fought this issue tooth and nail. A day after coming to power, the new chief minister of the state, Uddhav Thackeray, stayed the construction of the car shed, cut off its funding, and constituted a high-level panel of IAS officers to suggest an alternative spot for the shed. In January 2020, the committee submitted the report, which recommended that shifting the location of the car shed was not viable due to logistical hurdles and cost escalations. Eventually, in October 2020, the chief minister announced that the location of the shed would be shifted to Kanjurmarg – a piece of marshy land.

The decision on the new location faced immediate opposition and a tonne of criticism. Not only would stabilizing the marshy land extend the time of the construction by two years, but it was also contested that the title of the land is unclear. It was clear that if a legal contention remained, as it had been in 2015 in the Bombay High Court, the project would be delayed further. Fadnavis reacted to this decision by posting on Twitter that the high court had asked the government to deposit ₹2,661 crores (that is, the ready reckoner price) if the claims were settled in the future. As per documents of the technical committee appointed by the Maha Vikas Aghadi, the burden on the state exchequer for stopping work on the metro construction is about ₹5.87 crores per day. By this time, 30 per cent of the construction work had already been completed at the original site, which in terms of expenditure amounted to ₹400 crores. The staying of the project until October 2020 thus resulted in a delay of two and a half years and in an increased expense of ₹5,356 crores – ₹400 crores in scrapping the work carried out at the original Aarey site and ₹2,400 crores to be deposited if the land dispute remains unresolved.[9] A project that was estimated to cost about ₹25,000 crores has already seen an exponential increase in the cost by ₹8,000 crores, which will eventually hit the commuters in the form of ticket pricing, thus making the project financially impractical.

Another project that was scrapped was Fadnavis's proposal for a 'hyperloop' project to connect Mumbai and Pune, which would reduce the current travel time between the two cities from 4 hours to about 25 minutes. The Shiv Sena had not objected to the project when it was inked, however, the NCP had at the time heavily criticized the project, calling it an expensive experiment.[10] Keeping the interests of the Sena's new allies in mind, Uddhav Thackeray put the project 'under review' of a technical team and announced that a decision on it would be made after the completion of the review. Immediately after they decided to scrap it, Richard Branson, the owner of Virgin (the service provider for the project), came to meet Uddhav. After a couple of meetings with him, the Sena gave the project a second lease of life.[11]

When it came to the Ratnagiri Refinery and Petrochemicals Limited, as a part of the previous government the Shiv Sena had fought the BJP aggressively, opposing the project, stating that it would cause environmental havoc in the Konkan region.[12] The largest refinery of its kind, this was a pet project of the Union government. Amidst reports that the project would be shifted out of Maharashtra, the local leaders of the Shiv Sena allegedly held meetings with the involved parties, indicating that they were still interested in proceeding with the project as planned.[13] However, they were later officially reprimanded by the party for doing so. In mid-February 2020, an advertisement appeared in *Saamna* that read, 'Every step taken by the Ratnagiri refinery is in the interest of the future of the Konkan.' Although the Shiv Sena has denied changing its stance on the project, this endorsement in its mouthpiece contradicts that claim.[14]

COVID-19

Even as the Maha Vikas Aghadi was walking on eggshells on several issues, the COVID-19 pandemic struck the world, and India was no exception. Maharashtra was particularly badly hit. Maharashtra reported its first case on 9 March 2020, but by the end of the month the state was already at 300 cases, and Mumbai, India's commercial capital, and its metropolitan areas were among the worst hit. In only a month, the case count reached 1,297 in the state, with a mortality rate double that of the rest of the country.

At such a critical point, when crowd control was key in keeping the pandemic in check, the sudden lockdown announced by the central government rendered nearly 38 lakh migrants in the state jobless. Out of these 38 lakh, over 10 lakh migrants were working in Mumbai alone. Unable to survive without daily wages, the migrants became antsy and began to find ways to return to their home states and native villages. The shutdown of interstate and local transport, however, made their return impossible. In such a situation, government rations would have been the only way for them to feed themselves and their families. However, a survey conducted by the Stranded Workers Action Network showed that an alarming 96 per cent of migrants in the state of Maharashtra had no access to government ration and about 69 per cent would have run out of rations in a day.[15] One of the main reasons for this is that they did not possess local ration cards which would provide access to the subsidized grain schemes of the government. In such a desperate situation for survival, thousands of migrant workers began to walk to their hometowns and villages by foot, forcing the government to set up temporary relief centres. However, the government was only able to set up 262 relief camps, which would cater to only 70,000 migrants out of a total of 38 lakh. In a situation like this, rumours that special trains were being started for migrants to be transported to their home states prompted thousands of them to collect at Bandra Terminus on 19 May 2020. An occurrence like this could have been prevented by the issuance of timely clarifications. Instead, it was allowed to become a super-spreader event. The police force on the ground, under the leadership of NCP's Anil Deshmukh, did not stop thousands of migrants from making their way to the station, indicating that the allies were not able to work in tandem even during a public health emergency. When the government finally did make arrangements for relief centres, it was much too late and the arrangements were inadequate, revealing the institution's apathy towards a vulnerable population.

As the disease spread, so did rampant mismanagement in the state. Due to the lack of coordination between the Maharashtra state government, the Centre, district authorities and municipal corporations, authorities at all levels issued separate rules and instructions, causing chaos and fear. A case in point was when the MCGM chief, Praveen Pardeshi, an IAS officer par excellence with 29 years of service and a celebrated disaster management expert, was unceremoniously transferred for overriding the government's notification on the opening of liquor shops.[16]

By May 2020, the city of Mumbai alone saw as many as 1,100-plus new cases being reported in a day, taking the number of total cases in the city to 33,000. The state numbers didn't look good either, with 60,000 reported cases and over 1,900 deaths.[17] As the disease tightened its grip on the city, Mumbai ran out of available hospital beds for severely ill patients both in public and private hospitals.[18] Disturbing images emerged on social media of dead bodies left unattended on beds adjacent to patients under treatment.[19] Horrific accounts surfaced of patients having to spend over 20 hours next to dead bodies, establishing the fact that the state and the local government had failed to manage the crisis.[20]

The Shiv Sena has been at the helm of the MCGM since 1985 and in fact its rise in politics is attributed to its control over the corporation. It would be natural for voters to assume that with over three decades of experience in overseeing the city's affairs, the Sena would easily be able to manage any disaster, using available resources. However, this was not the case. The rate of growth in cases in Mumbai was almost similar to the rate of growth in cases in the rest of the state. However, while the rest of the state increased testing to over 12,000 samples per day, the MCGM did not step up testing in the city despite having the capacity to do so.[21] Although the pandemic in itself was an unprecedented situation, out of all the states and major cities of the country, Mumbai and Maharashtra still remain the worst hit in the country. Perhaps a more experienced head of government would have taken more timely, appropriate decisions and maintained a tighter grip on the bureaucracy, to be able to keep the pandemic in check.

During the onset of the pandemic, Chief Minister Uddhav Thackeray used to address the state via social media platforms a few times a week in order to give an update on the COVID situation and instil hope in people. However, as time passed, his updates became sparse, infrequent and repetitive. He stopped stepping out of his house and had not, till the end of October 2020, toured the state even once to assess the ground reality, inviting veiled criticism from his ally Sharad Pawar.[22] Instead, he seems to have deputed his son Aaditya to do the job.[23] The problem with this arrangement is that Aaditya is inexperienced. Leaders within the Sena, the NCP as well as the Congress have publicly expressed reservations about his role in the government.

Within the Shiv Sena echelons, his growing stature has ruffled the feathers of many old-timers and a power struggle looms large.[24] In the initial months of governance, his presence at all the meetings, regardless of the department, was seen as the enthusiasm of a newbie. However, it has been reported that it is now perceived by others within the party as downright interference. 'No other minister attends the meetings of other departments or holds meetings with other departments. He is holding meetings across the board. Why? Are the rest of us incapable?' asked a senior minister of the Congress.

'He is young and enthusiastic, and is helping his father,' said an NCP minister, 'but', he added, 'it will concern us if he is on the throne.'

A senior leader of the Shiv Sena put it this way, 'His elevation is a message to Eknath Shinde that Aaditya Thackeray is the second-in-command in the Shiv Sena. There will be a power tussle within the Shiv Sena. Eknath Shinde cannot be pushed aside.'[25]

From the beginning of 2020, observers have begun to wonder if the Maha Vikas Aghadi is in self-destruct mode and whether the three allies are so disconnected from each other that running a functional government is proving to be difficult for them.

If the alliance fails, the Shiv Sena has the most to lose among the three parties. In being a part of the current alliance, the Shiv Sena has seemingly abandoned the party's central ideology on which Balasaheb had built its popularity – the ideology that remains the glue that binds most of its workers. As of today, it is no different from the NCP and has little that is different from the other political parties to offer to the voter. While it would make most sense for the Sena to focus on a developmental agenda, the party remains mired in ideological differences, petty fights with rivals and is struggling with the management of the pandemic and reviving the economy of the state. Even Sena insiders have begun to worry about this identity crisis. They worry that they will not be able to sway the voters come election time.[26] Even when talks of the formation of a tripartite government were going on, they had raised issues with Uddhav about not being able to explain their political flip-flop to their constituents.

If the alliance shows any indication of failure, not only will Shiv Sena loyalists begin to abandon the party, but the party will also find it hard to acquire new members. It is, in fact, rival parties who will benefit the most from the Sena's shrunken voter base. While the Congress is insignificant in the current equation because of its heavy dependence on its alliance partners to whom it is indebted for being in power despite getting the least number of seats among the four parties, a regional party like the NCP will gain hugely from the Sena's mistakes because they will be able to lure voters who don't vote based on ideology. A strong right-wing party, like the BJP, stands to gain the most because it will appeal to voters loyal to a clear right-wing agenda and still holds the people's mandate as the party with the largest number of seats.

NOTES

Prologue

1. '"Make me CM", Beed farmer asks Governor as Maharashtra deals with BJP–Sena differences', *Hindustan Times*, 1 November 2019.
2. Government of India, 'Damage to crops in Maharashtra due to unseasonal rains', Relief Web, 6 December 2019.
3. 'Declare wet drought in Maharashtra: Aaditya Thackeray to Governor', *Free Press Journal*, 1 November 2019.
4. 'When politicians in Maharashtra suddenly remembered farmers', *Week*, 25 November 2019.
5. Ibid.
6. Ibid.
7. 'Devendra Fadnavis's first signature of new term was on this cheque', Ed. Shylaja Varma, NDTV, 26 November 2019.
8. Jayashree Bhosale, 'Onion price may stay high till Jan', *Economic Times*, 4 December 2019.

1. Chanakya Meets the Vizier

1. Monica Aggarwal, 'Uddhav Thackeray's Shiv Sena ropes in Prashant Kishor to strategize for Maharashtra assembly elections,

Aaditya Thackeray to be pitched as "new hope"', Republic World, 15 July 2019.

'Prashant Kishor real kingmaker of Shiv Sena–NCP–Cong Alliance? Details here', Republic World, 22 November 2019.

2. Name changed.
3. Sanjay Jog, 'Nilesh Rane levels serious charges against Bal Thackeray', *DNA India*, 16 January 2019.
4. Vinaya Deshpande, 'The curious case of Palghar seat and why it's become prestige battle between Shiv Sena, BJP', CNN News18, 26 March 2019.
5. 'Amit Shah meets Uddhav Thackeray; Shiv Sena–BJP may announce alliance to continue,' Outlook India, 18 February 2019.
6. 'Balasaheb Thackeray in Aap Ki Adalat (Full Interview)', YouTube, uploaded by India TV, 28 November 2014.
7. Chaitanya Marpakwar, 'Rise of Milind Narvekar: From Uddhav Thackeray's personal assistant to Shiv Sena party secretary', *Mumbai Mirror*, 24 January 2018.
8. Vicky Nanjappa, 'Between 2015–17, Shiv Sena saw a dip in donations by 70 per cent', One India, 7 August 2018.
9. Ashish Dikshit, 'Illegitimate child, alleged fraud: Thackeray sons battle over will', *Quint*, 21 July 2016.
10. 'From receptionist to powerful socialite, Smita Thackeray has come a long way', *India Today*, 30 November 1999; Samyabrata Ray Goswami and Sanjay K. Jha, 'Defiant daughterin-law adds to Sena woes', *Telegraph India*, 19 November 2009.
11. 'BJP, Shiv Sena announce alliance for Lok Sabha elections', *India Today*, 18 February 2019.
12. 'Maharashtra Assembly Polls 2014: MNS ends, Asaduddin Owaisi's Majli-e-Ittehadul Muslimeen makes entry with 2 wins', *Economic Times*, 20 October 2014.
13. 'How Raj Thackeray's campaign is helping Congress and NCP', *Money Control*, 19 April 2019.

14. 'Lok Sabha Election 2019: Raj Thackeray's "lav re toh video" a big hit this poll season', *DNA India*, 2 May 2019.
15. Jeetendra Dixit, 'All parties have been using Raj Thackeray for two decades', ABP News, 10 February 2020.
16. Election Commission of India, www.eci.gov.in.
17. Krishna Kumar, 'Raj Thackeray meets Sonia Gandhi', *Economic Times*, 8 July 2019.

2. Sleeping with the Enemy

1. 'Shiv Sena will contest 2019 Assembly and Lok Sabha elections solo, no alliance with BJP', *Scroll*, 23 January 2018.
2. 'Shiv Sena echoes Rahul Gandhi, attacks PM Modi on Rafale', *Times of India*, 10 February 2019.
3. Kamlesh Damodar Sutar, 'Uddhav Thackeray attacks PM Modi over demonitisation, says shedding tears on TV not enough', *India Today*, 24 November 2016.
4. 'Shiv Sena criticizes Modi's promise to reclaim black money', *India Today*, 28 June 2016.
5. Prafulla Marpakwar, Bhavika Jain and Ambarish Mishra, 'Maharashtra CM post must be shared, says Uddhav Thackeray; Shiv Sena threatens pullout', *Times of India*, 21 February 2019.
6. 'BJP is ready for any method of polls', *Bridge Chronicle*, 3 August 2019.
7. 'Chandrakant Patil gets Revenue, MoS Home for Shiv Sena', *Outlook*, 10 July 2016.
8. 'Maha twist: Sharad Pawar's NCP offers outside support to BJP, Shiv Sena waiting in the wings', *India Today*, 19 October 2014.
9. Mrityunjay Bose, 'Shiv Sena mounts pressure on BJP, distribute AB forms', *Deccan Herald*, 29 September 2019.
10. Viju B., 'Maharashtra minister's lie nailed', *Times of India*, 8 September 2006.

11. G. Mohiuddin Jeddy, 'Refused BJP ticket from Belapur, Ganesh Naik may contest from Airoli', *Hindustan Times*, 2 October 2019.
12. 'Trouble for Shiv Sena after 200 party members quit over Navi Mumbai Assembly seats being offered to BJP's Ganesh Naik', *Firstpost*, 1 October 2019.

3. Ramping up for the Battle

1. 'Politics over a scam', *Frontline*, 25 October 2019.
2. 'Won't bow down before Delhi, ready for ED hospitality on Sept 27: Sharad Pawar', *India Today*, 25 September 2019.
3. Ibid.
4. 'ED says Sharad Pawar is not required to visit office but he is firm to go: NCP leader', YouTube, uploaded by ANI News, 27 September 2019.
5. 'ED may not allow Sharad Pawar to enter its Mumbai office on Friday', *Federal*, 26 September 2019.
6. 'Sharad Pawar drops plan to visit ED office after meeting Mumbai Police Commissioner', *Economic Times*, 27 September 2019.
7. Ibid.
8. 'Explained: Rs 25,000 crore Maharashtra Cooperative Bank Scam in which Sharad Pawar is a key accused', *Swarajya*, 27 September 2019; Ketaki Ghoge, 'All about the MSC Bank scam', *Hindustan Times*, 25 September 2019.
9. Chaitanya Marpakwar, 'Ajit Pawar asked son Parth to think about quitting politics', *Pune Mirror*, 29 September 2019.
10. Mustafa Shaikh, 'Resigned as Sharad Pawar was defamed because of me: Ajit Pawar', *India Today*, 28 September 2019.
11. Prachee Kulkarni, 'Ajit Pawar quit as he is upset over my name in MSCB case', *Pune Mirror*, 28 September 2019.
12. Ibid.

13. 'ED case against Pawar has galvanized NCP ahead of polls: Sanjay Raut', Press Trust of India, 27 September 2019.
14. 'Indira Gandhi used to meet gangster Karim Lala: Sanjay Raut', Press Trust of India, 15 January 2019.
15. Saurabh Gupta, 'Sena Leader withdraws "Indira Gandhi met don Karim Lala" remark after row, NDTV, 16 January 2020.
16. 'Devendra Fadnavis Exclusive: Assesses his term and on why he is fit for position', YouTube, uploaded by India Today Conclave, 22 September 2019.
17. 'BJP will get 3/4th majority in Maha: Amit Shah', Press Trust of India, 22 September 2019.
18. 'BJP–Sena alliance will be a huge advantage, says Fadnavis', *India Today*, 4 October 2019.
19. 'CM Devendra Fadnavis confirms Narayan Rane to join cabinet', *Times of India*, 18 October 2019.
20. Abhiram Ghadyalpatil, 'Maharashtra: Unease grows in BJP over Narayan Rane's likely cabinet entry', *Mint*, 31 October 2017.
21. Shiv Kumar, 'Pawar Play', *Tribune*, 27 October 2019.
22. Omkar Khandekar, 'How the Shiv Sena ensured Aaditya Thackeray's election victory', *Mint*, 1 November 2019.
23. Election Commission of India, Maharashtra Legislative Assembly Election 2019, www.eci.gov.in/files/file/11699.

4. D-Day

1. Omkar Khandekar, 'How the Shiv Sena ensured Aaditya Thackeray's election victory', *Mint*, 1 November 2019.
2. 'Aaditya Thackeray is a visionary leader says Arvind Sawant', *Deccan Chronicle*, 11 November 2019.
3. 'Will ensure 6th floor office for Aaditya Thackeray in Mantralaya says Sanjay Raut', *Times of India*, 30 September 2019.

4. Ahsan Abbas, 'Uddhav Thackeray wants Shiv Sainik as Maharashtra CM, BJP says no harm in expressing desire', Zee News, 7 October 2019.
5. 'Devendra Fadnavis will be seen sitting next to Uddhav Thackeray in Shiv Sena's next Dussehra rally: Sanjay Raut', Zee News, 9 October, 2019.
6. Pavan Dahat, 'How Devendra Fadnavis cut down rivals and weakened allies to dominate Maharashtra politics', *Huffington Post*, 17 October 2019.
7. 'BJP insiders defeated my daughter Rohini Khadse and Pankaja Munde claims Eknath Khadse', *HW News*, 5 December 2019.
8. 'Mehta found guilty in Lokayukta inquiry', *Bridge Chronicle*, 7 June, 2019.
9. 'Maharashtra minister Vinod Tawde accused of scam, denies charges', *Hindustan Times*, 30 June 2015.
10. 'Had set out for more seats in Maharashtra says Sharad Pawar', NDTV, 24 October 2019.
11. 'Maharashtra memory lane: When Sharad Pawar offered to support a BJP govt', *India Today*, 2 November 2019.
12. '2014 support offer was "ploy" to keep Sena away from the BJP: Sharad Pawar', NDTV, 13 July 2020.
13. 'Uddhav Thackeray pushes for 50:50 formula for CM's post', *India Today*, 24 October 2019.
14. Sudhir Suryawanshi, *Checkmate: How the BJP Won and Lost Maharashtra*, New Delhi: Penguin Random House, 2020.
15. Swati Chaturvedi, 'In Aaditya Thackeray's promotion, the role of mother Rashmi', NDTV, 30 December 2019.
16. Vishwas Waghmode, 'Rashmi Thackeray: Mrs Surefire', *Indian Express*, 8 March 2020.

5. Permutations and Combinations

1. 'Posters depicting Aaditya Thackeray as Maharashtra CM surface in Mumbai's Worli', Zee News, 25 October 2019.
2. 'Young Soch Wins: Posters celebrating Aaditya Thackeray's electoral victory appear in Prabhadevi', Asian News International, 26 October 2019.
3. 'Uddhav Thackeray calls meeting with Shiv Sena leaders on government formation, BJP to discuss about 50:50 formula', Zee News, 26 October 2019.
4. Suchitra Karthikeyan, 'Tiger with clock sniffs lotus in Shiv Sena's party symbol-filled post', Republic World, 25 October 2019.
5. '"Remote Control of power" in Maharashtra with Shiv Sena: Sanjay Raut tells BJP', Zee News, 27 October 2019.
6. 'IRS Q1 2019: Lokmat rules Maharashtra, Gujarat Samachar leader in Gujarat', Exchange4media, 1 May 2019.
7. 'Shiv Sena not promised CM's post for 2.5 years: Devendra Fadnavis', *Times of India*, 29 October 2019.
8. Krishnat Patil, 'Congress, NCP MLAs in touch with Shiv Sena, claims Sanjay Raut', Zee News, 31 October 2019.
9. Tushar Dhara, 'We got less number of seats but won't play second fiddle to anybody: Prithviraj Chavan', *Caravan*, 30 October 2019.
10. 'Sena wanted to form govt in alliance with Congress after 2014 Maharashtra polls: Prithviraj Chavan', *Times of India*, 20 January 2020.

6. The Sena Switches Sides

1. Suchitra Karthikeyan, 'BMC removes "Maha CM only Aaditya Thackeray" posters outside Matoshree', Republic World, 31 October 2019.

2. 'Maharashtra: Is President in your pocket? Sena edit on Mungantiwar', *Economic Times*, 2 November 2019.
3. 'Is President in your pocket? Shiv Sena lashes out at BJP over Maharashtra govt conundrum', *Times Now*, 2 November 2019.
4. Ehsan Abbas, 'NCP ready to support Shiv Sena to form government in Maharashtra, say sources', Zee News, 10 November 2019.
5. 'NCP chief Sharad Pawar meets Sonia Gandhi, says "responsibility of BJP–Shiv Sena to form govt in Maharashtra"', Zee News, 4 November 2019.
6. 'Shiv Sena will not be an obstacle in government formation in Maharashtra: Sanjay Raut after meeting Governor Bhagat Singh Koshiyari', Zee News, 4 November 2019.

7. Catch-22

1. Chaitanya Marpakwar, 'Power has a new address: Matoshree loses its monopoly to South Mumbai', *Mumbai Mirror*, 28 November 2019.
2. 'Sharad Pawar dares Amit Shah to form government in Maharashtra, rules out possible alliance with Shiv Sena', Zee News, 6 November 2019.
3. Ramraje Shinde, 'Amit Shah unwilling to give Maharashtra CM, Home Minister post to Shiv Sena: Sources', Zee News, 4 November 2019.
4. 'Maharashtra: Shiv Sena divided over support to BJP; one faction wants deadlock to end, other adamant on 50:50 formula', Zee News, 7 November 2019.

8. New Beginnings

1. Nilesh Shukla, 'Maharashtra govt distributing "packets" to remain in power: Shiv Sena accuses BJP of poaching new MLAs', Zee News, 7 November 2019.

2. 'Maharashtra deadlock: BJP attempts to end differences with Shiv Sena, sends Sambhaji Bhide to meet Uddhav Thackeray', Zee News, 8 November 2019.
3. 'Devendra Fadnavis' press conference after resigning as Maharashtra CM', *Print*, 8 November 2019.
4. 'Uddhav Thackeray Holds Press Conference', *Quint*, 8 November 2019.
5. Chaitanya Marpakwar, 'Sena asks for police protection for its MLAs; writes to CP, DGP', *Mumbai Mirror*, 9 November 2019.

9. Games Governors Play

1. Shubhangi Kumari Singh, 'If Shiv Sena votes against BJP in House, will consider supporting them: NCP president Nawab Malik', Zee News, 9 November 2019.
2. 'Shiv Sena likely to stake claim to form government in Maharashtra on Monday; Sanjay Raut may meet Congress leaders in Delhi', Zee News, 11 November 2019.
3. 'President Kovind accepts Shiv Sena MP Arvind Sawant's resignation, gives portfolio to Prakash Javadekar', Zee News, 12 November 2019.
4. Sudhir Suryawanshi, *Checkmate: How the BJP Won and Lost Maharashtra*, New Delhi: Penguin Random House, 2020.
5. 'The Sharad Pawar–Sonia Gandhi phone call that thwacked Shiv Sena's plans', NDTV, 12 November 2020; Sahil Joshi, 'NCP letter behind Prez rule? Sharad Pawar move brings Shiv Sena, Congress closer', *India Today*, 13 November 2019.

10. President's Rule

1. 'President's rule imposed in Maharashtra; Congress cries foul, Sena moves SC', *National Herald*, 12 November 2019.

2. Sahil Joshi, 'NCP letter behind Prez rule? Sharad Pawar move brings Shiv Sena, Congress closer', *India Today*, 13 November 2019.

11. Powar Power

1. Misha Bhatt, 'Some Balasaheb Thackeray quotes that Shiv Sena must remind itself of', Republic World, 11 November 2019.
2. 'Congress calls Shiv Sena "Desi Taliban"', *Hindustan Times*, 13 October 2015.
3. Navika Kumar, 'Was the waiting game necessary?', *Times of India*, 13 November 2019.
4. '"I will not go along with a scoundrel": When Bal Thackeray refused to ally with NCP', *Free Press Journal*, 13 November 2019.
5. Ravi Tripathi, 'Sena, NCP to share Maha CM post for 2.5 years each; Supriya Sule is Sharad Pawar's top choice: Sources', *DNA India*, 21 November 2019.
6. Kaveree Bamzai, 'Supriya Sule was the Darling of Lutyens' Delhi, but is now Maharashtra's very own tai', *Print*, 29 November 2019.
7. Shruti Ganpatye, 'Most NCP MLAs "return", say Ajit Pawar duped them', Mumbai Mirror, 24 November 2019.
8. Makarand Gadgil and Shruti Ganpatye, 'Operator on the line: How Ajit Pawar's stealth attack was engineered', *Mumbai Mirror*, 24 November 2019.
9. Sahil Joshi, 'Power coup to Pawarplay: Devendra Fadnavis on his 80-hr stint as Maharashtra CM', *India Today*, 12 December 2019.
10. 'Uddhav "ready" to be CM after Pawar says Sena chief unanimous choice', *Times of India*, 22 November 2019.
11. Makarand Gadgil and Shruti Ganpatye, 'Operator on the line: How Ajit Pawar's stealth attack was engineered', *Mumbai Mirror*, 24 November 2019.

12. A Midnight Coup

1. '"Party and Family Split" Supriya Sule's WhatsApp Status Confirms Split Within NCP', YouTube, uploaded by IndiaTV, 22 November 2019.
2. 'Ajit Pawar a traitor: Shiv Sena's Sanjay Raut on Maharashtra deal', *India Today*, 23 November 2019.
3. 'Maharashtra: Behind Tuesday's smiles, some anxious moments', *Indian Express*, 27 November 2019.
4. Sudhir Suryawanshi, 'How Sonia saved this govt', *Mumbai Mirror*, 18 May 2020.
5. Pavan Dahat, 'How Sharad Pawar destroyed BJP, Ajit Pawar's Maharashtra hopes in 48 hours', *Huffington Post*, 27 November 2019.
6. 'My bungalow is open house. At times, it's like a bus stand: Dhananjay Munde', *Indian Express*, 26 November 2019.

13. Show of Strength

1. Iram Siddiqui, 'Holed up in brother's Mumbai flat, Ajit Pawar meets emissaries from NCP all day', *Indian Express*, 24 November 2019.
2. Pavan Dahat, 'How Sharad Pawar destroyed BJP, Ajit Pawar's Maharashtra hopes in 48 hours', *Huffington Post*, 27 November 2019.
3. Faisal Malik and Naresh Kamath, 'NCP, Sena, Congress MLAs gather together in show of strength', *Hindustan Times*, 26 November 2019.

14. The Court Intervenes

1. Pavan Dahat, 'How Sharad Pawar destroyed BJP, Ajit Pawar's Maharashtra hopes in 48 hours', *Huffington Post*, 27 November 2019.

15. A Government in (In)Action

1. Saurubh Gupta, 'Did Uddhav Thackeray Get Trolled by Deputy Ajit Pawar? NCP Denies It', NDTV, 27 July 2020.
2. 'Maharashtra will go ahead with CAA, NPR says Uddhav Thackeray after meeting PM Modi', *Times of India*, 22 February 2020.
3. 'Signs of cracks in Maharashtra alliance over CAA, NPR; Pawar says "Will Try to Convince Thackeray"', *Outlook*, 18 February 2020.
4. Anupama Katakam, 'Elgar Parishad case: victims of vendetta', *Frontline*, 28 August 2020.
5. 'Sharad Pawar criticises Uddhav Thackeray for letting NIA probe Elgar Parishad case', *English Jagran*, 15 February 2020.
6. 'Maharashtra to provide 5% quota to Muslims in education: Minority affairs minister Nawab Malik', *Times of India*, 28 February 2020.
7. 'No decision on Muslim quota yet', *Times of India*, 2 March 2020.
8. 'My name is not "Rahul Savarkar", will never apologize for truth: Rahul Gandhi', *Economic Times*, 14 December 2019.
9. Tweet by Devendra Fadnavis, 11 October 2020.
10. Prachee Kulkarni, 'Mumbai–Pune Hyperloop may get scrapped; Shiv Sena says decision to be taken post review', *Pune Mirror*, 5 December 2019.
11. 'Uddhav Thackeray's second lease of life for Hyperloop', *Tribune*, 4 March 2020.
12. 'Shiv Sena opposed Nanar refinery project as "sons of the soil" were against it: Aaditya Thackeray', Press Trust of India, 18 September 2019.
13. Shoumojit Banerjee, 'Toe party line on Nanar refinery or face action: Sena to members', *The Hindu*, 2 March 2020.
14. Amey Tirodkar, 'Is the "Nanar Refinery" back? The curious case of Shiv Sena's flip-flops', Newsclick, 15 February 2020.

15. Priyanka Kakodkar, 'No govt rations for 96% of migrants in Maharashtra: Survey', *Times of India*, 11 May 2020.
16. Lyla Bavadam, 'Mumbai Municipal Commissioner transferred as COVID-19 cases increase sharply', *Frontline*, 9 May 2020.
17. 'Maharashtra's COVID-19 tally rises to 2,84,281 with record spike of 8,641', *DNA India*, 16 July 2020.
18. Jyoti Shelar, 'Mumbai runs out of beds in ICUs, patients suffer', *The Hindu*, 16 April 2020.
19. Lata Mishra, 'Unattended bodies in Sion hospital ward traumatise patients', *Mumbai Mirror*, 8 May 2020.
20. Alka Dhupkar and Satish Malavade, 'Cooper patient spends 22 hours with bodies to his left and right', *Mumbai Mirror*, 24 April 2020.
21. Sahil Joshi, 'Coronavirus: Why is Mumbai's testing number stuck at 4,000 per day?', *India Today*, 12 June 2020.
22. Faisal Malik, 'CM expected to travel across state, but Uddhav yet to start tours: Pawar', *Hindustan Times*, 29 July 2020.
23. Ranjeet Jadhav, 'Aaditya Thackeray: I am 100 per cent ready to lead the state', *Mid-Day*, 13 October 2019.
24. Haima Deshpande, 'Shiv Sena scion Aaditya Thackeray takes lead role in govt matters and not all are pleased', *Print*, 20 July 2020.
25. Chaitanya Marpakwar, 'NCP stealing the show taking unilateral decisions: Sena ministers tell CM Thackeray', *Mumbai Mirror*, 11 July 2020.
26. Ibid.

ACKNOWLEDGEMENTS

Many people have, directly and indirectly, been instrumental in bringing this book to life and I possibly cannot end this book without thanking them.

My heartfelt gratitude to Mr and Mrs Narayan Rane, for your constant love, strength and support. If I am able to fly, it is because you have given me the wings. I will remain forever indebted to you.

A big shout-out to my friend and agent, Anish Chandy, for his advice and honest feedback. There is no better sounding board. You are truly the best literary agent in the country.

Thank you to the fabulous team at Hachette India, especially Poulomi Chatterjee and Sini Nair, for helping me take this story from idea to execution in the smoothest possible way.

The cover wouldn't be this beautiful if it wasn't for Nisha Nainani's initial ideas, which then were converted to perfection by Haitenlo Semy.

All credits for the impactful and fabulous trailer go to Vivek Joshi. Your creativity, my friend, is unparalleled.

Thank you, Sidharth Jain, for recognizing the strength of the story for screen adaptation. I have no doubt in your capabilities to turn it into a very successful original series.

There are many political leaders whom I can't name to protect their confidentiality. However, I am deeply thankful to each of you. I am thankful to your support teams as well for ensuring clear communication channels.

Finally, writing and bringing out a difficult book like this calls for immense support from those closest to you. My family and friends have stood by me through the toughest of times and helped me make decisions when I was torn. Thank you, all, for being there. Each one of you holds a very special place in my heart.

Priyam Gandhi-Mody is a strategist specializing in political advocacy and brand building. An advanced understanding of state affairs and a tenacious ability to build high-profile networks enable her to implement effective political communication strategies. While she is happy to be busy analysing politics, she ensures that she finds time to write, especially about her unique experiences and the interesting people she encounters in her profession.